SOME ASPECTS OF
ANCIENT INDIAN CULTURE

SOME ASPECTS OF
ANCIENT INDIAN CULTURE

Sir William Meyer Lectures, 1938-39

BY

D. R. BHANDARKAR

GYAN

Published by

Gyan Publishing House
5, Ansari Road
Daryaganj, New Delhi-110002
Phone: 011-47034999, 9811692060
E-mail: books@gyanbooks.com

Distribution Network
gyanbooks.com
India, USA, Canada, UK, Australia

ISBN: 978-93-6280-297-2 (HB)
First Published, 1940

2nd Impression 2024

Printed at: Gyan Press, Delhi.

SOME ASPECTS OF ANCIENT INDIAN CULTURE
Author: D. R. BHANDARKAR

SOME ASPECTS OF
ANCIENT INDIAN CULTURE

Sir William Meyer Lectures, 1938–39

D. R. BHANDARKAR

UNIVERSITY OF MADRAS

SOME ASPECTS OF
ANCIENT INDIAN CULTURE

Sir William Meyer Lectures, 1938–39

BY

D. R. BHANDARKAR, M.A., (HONY.) PH.D., F.R.A.S.B.,
&c., &c.

UNIVERSITY OF MADRAS

1940

INTRODUCTION

It is impossible for me to thank sufficiently the Syndicate of the University of Madras for having invited me to deliver the course of Sir William Meyer (Endowment) Lectures for 1938-39. Such a thing is considered to be a great honour which that University can confer upon a scholar. The invitation, however, came at a time when I was very busy with my Presidential Address and other work connected with the Indian History Congress which came off at Allahabad in October 1938. I could not therefore decide quickly whether I should accept it. On May 31st, 1936, I had to retire as Carmichael Professor, Calcutta University, where the late Sir Asutosh Mookerjee, the greatest Indian of his time, had permanently transferred me from the Archaeological Department. It was true that when I was in this Department, I came in direct contact with many monuments of Ancient India which fascinated me most. But it was also true that the administrative work of the Department prevented my devoting my undivided attention to the study of the history and culture of Ancient India. I was therefore very much delighted when the Vikramāditya of the modern age brought me to the Calcutta University. I at once turned my attention to the critical study of such subjects as the Ancient Polity of India, the Cultural History of the pre-Mauryan period, the Position of Woman in Ancient India, the Origin and Development of Caste, and so forth, and so on. The first of these subjects I had to tackle when at the instance of Pandit Madan Mohan Malaviyaji and Dr. A. B. Dhruva I delivered before the Benares Hindu University the Manindra Chandra Nandy Lectures, 1925, on 'Some Aspects of Ancient Hindu Polity.' In regard to the other subjects, I had prepared full notes with a view to continue my Carmichael Lectures Series soon after the completion of my sixtieth year when a Research Professor is supposed to be most conversant with the subject of his life-long study. But owing to my retirement this object remained unfulfilled. When therefore the Syndicate of the Madras University invited me to deliver the Sir William Meyer Lectures, the idea struck me that one of the courses which I intended delivering before the Calcutta University after my sixtieth year I might deliver without much trouble before the Madras University. Accordingly I selected the Cultural History of the pre-Mauryan India as my subject and delivered these Lectures under the title " Some Aspects of Ancient Indian Culture."

It is a matter of exceeding gratification that this Lecturership is connected with Sir William Meyer, who was a Madras civilian. It has become a fashion now-a-days to decry a civilian, especially if he is a Britisher. But it is forgotten what invaluable services he has rendered to Indian literature and philology. We have only to consider the names of Sir James Campbell and A. M. T. Jackson of the Bombay, Sir Herbert Risley of the Bengal, and Sir Denzil Ibettson of the Panjab, Civil Service, to mention a few names only. But Sir William Meyer seems to have outshone his brother civilians, because he not only was a thoughtful writer but evinced a great and genuine interest in University education even in his retirement and for that purpose made a bequest which has resulted in the Lecturership instituted in his name by the Madras University. And as only scholars of well-established reputation are invited to deliver these Lectures, naturally I felt proud that I was done this honour. How far I have executed the task it is for others to determine. I would only add: *Guṇa-dōshau budhō gṛihṇann=indu-kshvēḍāv=iv=Ēśvaraḥ ; śirasā ślāghatē pūrvvaṁ paraṁ kaṇṭhē niyachchhati.*

In conclusion, it is first my duty to express my deep sense of gratitude for all the good turns, known and unknown, which Prof. Nilakanta Sastri has done me from the beginning to the end in connection with these Lectures. Secondly, I cannot also sufficiently thank the G. S. PRESS that has lightened the travails of my proof reading and has convinced me that an Indian-owned or Indian managed Press can be as good as any first-rate Press in Europe.

December, 1939. D. R. B.

CONTENTS

LECTURE I

ĀRYA, DĀSA AND ŚŪDRA

The subject of this course of Lectures is: Some Aspects of Ancient Indian Culture. This subject may not interest some of my countrymen assembled here this evening, especially those who are caught up in the vortex of politics. History of India, many of them still say, may wait, but Science and Economics cannot, if our country is to occupy a prominent place in the comity of nations. If any history is to be studied at all, they further assert, let us study the modern history of Europe and America peopled by the white nations who are at the pinnacle of civilisation, because of the development of Science and Economics amongst them. But a great historian from one of these continents has truly said that " the greater part of the social and intellectual structure of a nation is bequeathed to it by former generations, that unconscious tradition is perhaps the most potent agent in historical life, that the margin of change is surprisingly small and progressive nations quite exceptional." The traditions and past experiences of our country are thus a precious heritage which we should all carefully study and properly value, especially at a time when the alchemy of European culture is apparently transmuting, I do not know, whether into gold or brass, the socio-religious fabric of India beyond all recognition. Again, it was only the other day that I had occasion to draw the attention of the historians to what the great savant Max Müller has said in the first Lecture of the Series that he delivered in 1882 before the Cambridge University. " Why do we want to know history ?"—he enquires. Simply because, he replies, all of us ought to know " our own antecedents, our own ancestors, our own descent ;" in other words, the historian ought to tell us, and we ought to know, everything about our physical, intellectual and spiritual ancestry. It is therefore absolutely necessary that all Indians should be well conversant with this type of the History of India and that the Mussalmans and the Christians should be as much interested in the ancient period as the Hindus themselves.

Years ago, the German scholar, Prof. A. Ludwig, correctly said : " The Ṛig-Veda presupposes nothing of that which we know in Indian literature, while, on the other hand, the whole of Indian

I.C.—1

literature and the whole of Indian life presuppose the Veda,"[1] This fully justifies, remarked the late Prof. Winternitz, the general view of the great antiquity of the Ṛig-Veda, even of the "later" parts of it. And he accordingly ascribed the composition of this work to c. 2500 B.C.[2] The question that now arises is: What does the Rig-Veda primarily teach us? The reply that most of us will give is that the Ṛig-Veda tells us about the Aryan culture. But I am afraid, this is only half of the answer. Because the Ṛig-Veda teaches us about the non-Aryan culture also. And in that connection it has to be borne in mind that the Atharva-Veda also is of exceeding value. Further, we have to note that much depends upon the angle of vision from which we view things. Yāska, the author of the Nirukta, refers to four schools of studies which were prevalent in his time. Two of these were: (1) the Nairuktas or the School of the Etymologists to which he belonged and (2) the Aitihāsikas or the School of the Historians whose opinions he often thought worth quoting. In modern times also the European scholars, especially of the last generation, represent such a School of Nairuktas and frequently interpret the Vedic texts strictly from the philological point of view. There was, however, one scholar amongst them, the late Prof. Hillebrandt, who was not a mere philologist but also historian. We want more of such philologist-historians if we wish to understand the Vedic life aright and in full. Thus the generality of scholars are of the opinion that when the Ṛig-Veda was composed, the Aryans were settled in the Punjāb, the Saptasindhus or Sindhus as it was then called. It is not, however, so well-known that they were in occupation of a considerable part of Eastern Afganistan also. This is clear from the fact that such rivers and streams as the Kubhā or the Kābul, the Krumu or the Kurum, and the Gomati or the Gomal are referred to in the Ṛig-Veda. We also find mention of such tribes as the Pakthas surviving in the modern Pakthun of Eastern Afghanistan and the Gandhāris after whom later on the province of Gandhāra was known. Nay, some hymns of the Ṛig-Veda, especially the Sixth Maṇḍala, seems to have been composed when the Aryans were occupying some parts of Iran, as was so ably pointed out by Hillebrandt. He locates Divodāsa's conflict with the Panis, Dāsas and so forth in Arachosia.[3] He thus

1. *Der Rigveda,* Vol. III, p. 183.

2. *Some Problems of Indian Literature* (Cal. Uni. Readership Lectures), p. 20.

3. *Vedische Mythologie,* I, 97 *ff*.

identifies the Paṇis with the Parnians of Strabo, the Dāsas with Dahae, the Pārāvatas with the Parautai of Ptolemy, and Bṛishaya with the Barsacutns of Arrian, and, above all, the river Sarasvatī, where the battle took place, not with the Sarasvatī of the Panjāb, but with the Haraqaiti, that is, the Arghandab of Arachosia.[4] Similarly, Ludwig sees several references to the Parśus or Persians, and thinks that in one of them the Parśus are actually associated with the Pṛithus, or the Parthians. He also identifies Pārthava of RV. VI 27.8 with the Parthians. Similarly, the word or the name Mitajñu occurs at least thrice in the Ṛig-Veda.[5] Perhaps it would be too far-fetched to identify it with the Mitāni who were settled on the north-west of Elam and whose kings' inscriptions of about 1400 B.C. were found a short time ago at Boghāz-koi. But perhaps it would not be so far-fetched if we identify the Keśis with the Kassi or Kassites who in the eighteenth century before Christ invaded Babylonia, and were eminent horsemen. In many passages of the Ṛig-Veda *keśin* horses are mentioned where the word is taken every time in the sense of 'possessed of a mane.' This is meaningless and tautologous, because every horse is possessed of a mane. Besides, in some texts, the word *keśin* occurs by itself, e.g., in *RV*., III. 41.9, where also it obviously signifies 'a horse.' Just as Sindhu was originally noted for horses which were therefore called *saindhava*, the Keśin country may similarly have been the habitat of an equinine species for which reason they were called *keśins*. It may be further pointed out that the Śatapatha-Brāhmaṇa speaks of a people called Keśins whose king "is mentioned as learning from Khaṇḍika the atonement for a bad omen at the sacrifice."[6] The same Brāhmaṇa and the Jaiminīya-Upanishad Brāhmaṇa speak of a king called Keśin Dārbhya, whose people, the Keśins, were apparently a branch of the Pañchālas Evidently these Keśins seem to be the descendants of the Kassi or Kassites settled in India in the time of the Ṛig-Veda.

It will thus be seen that the composers of the hymns were living side by side not only with the people of the Saptasindhus but also with those of Afghanistan, Arachosia and even Iran. It is well-known that in the historical period whenever there was a general condition of unrest among the tribes of Central Asia, it caused a flood of tribal migration. This is just what happened

4. See Macdonell and Keith's *Vedic Index* under each name.
5. *RV*., III, 59, 3 ; VI, 32, 3 ; and VII, 95, 4.
6. *Vedic Index*, sub voce.

about the beginning of the Christian era, forcing southward and into India not only Bactrian Greeks but also the Śakas, Palhavas, Ābhīras, Kushāṇas and so forth. Similarly when, in the sixth century A.D., the turbulent Hūṇas penetrated India, they did not come singly but along with other tribes such as the Gurjaras, Chāhmans, Maitrakas and so on. Is it conceivable that the Aryans alone entered the Panjāb from their original home in perfect amity and concord and without having to fight with other tribes on the route they were pursuing? The struggle for supremacy between the Āryas and the Dāsas is a theme of many hymns in the Ṛig-Veda. This is not all. The Āryas were fighting not only with the Dāsas but also with the Āryas. Thus Ṛig-Veda VI. 33.3 says: " Both these our foes, (our) Dāsa and our Ārya enemies, hast thou, heroic Indra, destroyed........" Similarly Ṛig-Veda VII. 83.1 has: " Ye smote and slew the Dāsa and Ārya enemies and protected Sudās with your succour, O Indra-Varuṇa." Many such passages can be quoted to show that Indra killed the Āryas and Dāsas most impartially provided they were the foemen of his worshipper. Nay, one Ṛik (*RV.* IV. 30.18) bemoans that Indra slew Arṇa and Chitraratha on the yonder side of the Sarayu, although they were Āryas. We may proceed one step further and discuss who by extraction Sudās was that has been referred to in the last but one passage. He was of course the hero of the *dāśa-rājña* or ' Battle of Ten Kings ' fought on the Parushṇī, where there were Ārya and Dāsa allies on both the sides. But he was also the grandson of Divodāsa Atithigva. And Hillebrandt seems to be right in interpreting the name as the ' heavenly Dāsa ' and conjecturing that he was himself a Dāsa. In Ṛig-Veda VI. 61.1 & *ff.*, Divodāsa is said to have fought against the Paṇis, Pārāvatas and Bṛishaya, and we have already pointed out with what tribes of Arachosia Hillebrandt identifies them. Nay, the Sarasvatī where the battle was fought is also identified by him with the Haraqaiti of Arachosia. But in the time of his grandson Sudās, we have also seen, the Dāśa-rājña battle came off on the Parushṇī or Rāvī in the Panjāb. It appears that the kingdom of the Tṛitsu family of the Bharata tribe to which these kings pertained extended from Arachosia to the Panjāb as was the case in later times with the Achaemenian family to which Darius the Great belonged. And if in this region there were living multifarious peoples such as the Āryas, Dāsas, Paṇis, Pārāvatas and so on, how can we expect any one of them to be black in colour? And, in fact, the Dāsas or Dasyus have been identified by Zimmer, Meyer and Hillebrandt with the Dahae of the Caspian Steppes who are supposed to be closely allied in race and language with the Iranians.[7] What then becomes of that well-known text: *Yo Dāsaṁ varṇam=adharaṁ guh=ākaḥ* (RV., II. 12.4), 'who has swept away the base Dāsa colour.' This is one of the texts on the strength of which some scholars have argued that here the fair-coloured Āryas have been distinguished from the dark-complexioned aborigines.[8] The other passage is: *hatvī Dasyūn pra Āryaṁ varṇam=āvat* (RV., III. 34.9), 'he destroyed the Dasyus and protected the Aryan colour.' But does *varṇa* necessarily signify 'colour' in these texts? And even if it does, what is there to show that the Ārya colour is in this particular verse described as 'fair' or the Dāsa as dark? Both these passages may, on the other hand, be compared to a third one, namely, *Indraḥ samastu yajamānam=Āryaṁ*........*Manave śāsad=avratān tvachaṁ krishṇām=arandhayat* (RV., I. 130.8), "Indra who in a hundred ways has preserved the Ārya worshipper..........has subjected the dusky skin to the Manus." There is one more Ṛik which similarly refers to the dark complexion of the Dasyus, namely, Ṛig-Veda IX. 41. 1-2, adverted to in the sequel. 'The dusky skin' has been here mentioned and even contrasted with the Āryas who must therefore be presumed to be fair-skinned. The Āryas must have come in contact with this dusky race somewhere in the Panjāb. But is there any text in the Ṛig-Veda, above all, Maṇḍala VI., where the original Dāsas or Dahaē are described as possessed of dark skin? The mere use of the term *varṇa* is nothing. Even supposing that in the first two passages it signifies 'colour,' it does not show that the *varṇa* of the Dāsas referred to therein was black. For aught we know to the contrary, the original Dāsas may have belonged to the Iranian race. On the other hand, the word *varṇa* is taken by some scholars in a different sense. The authors of the *Vedic Index* e.g. have rendered it by 'caste.'[9] Perhaps it will be better to render it by 'order, confraternity.' In all probability, it denoted some socio-religious order. We have already noticed the text where the Ārya Yajamānas are spoken of. We may now consider another passage: *Vi jānīhy=Āryān=ye cha Dasyavo barhishmate randhayā śāsad=avratān* &c., (I. 51.8), "Distinguish well between the Āryas and those who are Dasyus; chastising those devoid of sacred rites, subject them to the sacrificer." Here the Dasyus are described as not observing the

7. *Ibid.*

8. Muir's *Sanskrit Texts*, Vol. II, p. 282; *Vedic Index*, Vol. II, p. 247, *n.* 1.

9. Vol. I, p. 65 and *n.* 8.

sacred rites and have therefore to be surrendered to the Āryas, who are here designated 'sacrificers.' Similarly, we have *pra ye gāvō na bhūrṇayas=tveshā ayāso akramuḥ | ghnantaḥ kṛishṇām=apa tvachaṁ||....sāhvāṁso dasyum=avratam||* (*RV.* IX. 41.1-2). "Active and bright have they come forth, impetuous in speed like bulls, chasing away the black skin. Quelling the Dasyus devoid of rites,......" Quite in consonance with this is the text: *Sūryaṁ dīvi rohayantaḥ sudānava Āryā vratā visṛijanto adhi kshami* (*RV.* X. 65.11). "those very bounteous (gods), mounting the sun to heaven (*and*) spreading Ārya rites over the earth." Many such passages can be culled together which point to an ardent desire on the part of the Āryas to disseminate everywhere their rites, in other words, their religion. We have thus a constant antithetic juxtaposition of the two names Ārya and Dāsa or Dasyu. They were hostile to each other principally on account of difference of stock and religion. Dāsa or Dasyu no doubt originally denoted the Dahae of the Caspian Steppes. They certainly could not have been of a dark complexion. Some of the Dāsas, such as Divodāsa and his descendants, seem to have embraced the Ārya religion and become Āryans. And in fact, about the same time the term Dāsa lost its particularistic ethnological significance and denoted any foreigners who did not practise the Ārya *vratas.* Similarly, Ārya also was originally an ethnographic term, denoting one specific race or tribe. The name is preserved in the well-known Arianē which was once a frontier province of India and survived as late as the time of Kalhaṇa who in his Rājataraṅgiṇī (IV. 367) refers to it as Āryāṇaka. The eastern boundary of Arianē is the Indus; and the southern, the Indian Ocean, from the mouth of the Indus to the Persian Gulf. The western limit is said to be an imaginary line drawn from the Caspian gates to Carmania. And it probably coincided with the kingdom of the Tṛitsu family of the Bharata clan to which Divōdāsa and Sudās belonged. Strabo mentions many nations by whom Arianē is inhabited, and one of them is the Arioi living side by side with the Drangai.[10] It is not unreasonable to infer that these Arioi correspond to the Āryas after whom the province was called Arianē. The Arioi however seem to be different from the Areianians mentioned by Dionysios,[11] who are apparently the Iranians. Further, it is worthy of note that there are two inscriptions of the feudatory Prathihāra family of Maṇḍōr, both dated V. S. 918, which speak of a people called Ārya or Ajja

10. McCrindle's *Ancient India*, p. 89.
11. *Ibid.*, p. 188.

situated somewhere in the present Jodhpur territory.[12] They look like an offshoot or remnant of the ancient Ārya race and appear to have come to India from Arianē along with the Hūṇas and Gurjaras in the sixth century A.D. and settled somewhere in Mārwāṛ in the ninth. As has happened in the case of many ancient races and tribes such as the Asuras, Ābhīras and Gurjaras, they seem to have survived in the shape of a tiny clan or people named the Āryas after the race was in the main absorbed in the Indian population.

When the Āryas were being settled down in the Saptasindhu region, they must have continued to employ for some time the term Dāsa to denote the foreigners or aboriginals of that region who were of a dark colour. We have thus one Rik of a somewhat dubious meaning: *Sa vṛitrahā Indraḥ kṛishṇa-yonīḥ Purandaro dāsīr=āirayad vi* &c., &c., (*RV.* II. 20.7). The expression *kṛishṇa-yonīḥ dāsīḥ* has been variously explained. Some translate it by "Dāsa hosts of black descent," some by "the servile hosts who dwelt in darkness" and so forth. It is also uncertain whether the non-Aryan tribes of the country are here intended, or the demons of air who dwell in the dark clouds. But, as pointed out above, there are at least two clear references to the dusky skin of the Dasyus. We have therefore to suppose that Dāsa was used by the Āryas settling down in India to signify foreigners or barbarians of a dusky complexion. But they could not have employed the term in this sense for a long time. Because before long we find the term Dāsa or Dasyu replaced by Śūdra for this purpose. But this point we will discuss shortly.

I have already remarked that there is some evidence to show that Ārya after all is the name of a race. In fact, Ārya corresponds to the Arioi of Arianē just as Dahae does to Dasyu or Dāsa. But there is another word of frequent occurrence in the Ṛig-Veda which may be considered in this connection. It is the word Manu. It no doubt signifies now 'the father of the human race.' Such was not, however, its signification in the Ṛig-Vedic times, when Manu denoted the father, not of the human race, but of the authors of the hymns. Thus Ṛig-Veda I. 114.2 says: "Whatever health and strength father Manu won by sacrifice may we, under thy guidance, gain, O! Rudra." Nay, in one Ṛik Manu has been styled, not merely 'father Manu' but '*our* father Manu' (*Manuḥ pitā naḥ*—RV., II. 33.13). If Manu is thus spoken of as

12. D. R. Bhandarkar's *A List of the Inscriptions of Northern India, etc.*, Nos. 31 and 32.

the progenitor of the worshippers, it is no wonder if the same persons are spoken of as his descendants. To take one instance, Ṛig-Veda III. 3.6 has : "Agni, together with the gods, and the children (*jantubhih*) of Manush, celebrating a multiform sacrifice with hymns."[13] In fact, there are many hymns of the Ṛig-Veda which clearly show that the authors of them not only regarded Manu as the first person by whom the sacrificial fire was kindled and the institutor of the ceremonial of worship but also looked upon him as the progenitor of their race, thereby calling themselves *Manor-apatya, Manushaḥ jantu, Manusho viś,* and so forth. Nay, the word Manu or Manush was used singly, sometimes in the singular and sometimes in the plural, to denote these followers of Manu, that is, the adherents of Manu's cult, just as Śākya means not only Gautama Buddha but also a Buddhist mendicant. Two instances will suffice. Thus Ṛig-Veda V. 2.12 has *barhishmatē manave śarma yaṁsad havishmate manave śarma yaṁsat.* "To the Manus who spread the grass, i.e. who sacrifice, may he (=Agni) grant shelter; to the Manus who offer oblations may he grant shelter." In this text the word Manu has been used in the singular. But Ṛig-Vedas X. 91·9 has; *Yad devayanto dadhati payāṁsi te havishmanto manavo vṛikta-barhishaḥ,* "when these pious Manus, sacrificing and spreading the (sacrificial) grass, offer thee (=Agni) oblation." Here the word Manu has been used in the plural in the above text. Manu in these quotations stands not for the progenitor of the Aryan stock but rather of their religion. Hence they are styled Manus, the chosen race, to which the authors of the hymns believed themselves to belong. If any further proof is needed, it is furnished by the following Ṛiks. Thus Ṛig-Veda VI. 21.11 has: *Ye manuṁ chakrur=uparaṁ dāsāya,* "(gods) who made the Manus superior to the Dāsas." But perhaps the most appropriate Ṛik bearing on this point is the one which has already been cited in another connection but will bear repetition here: *Indraḥ samastu Yajamānam=Āryam......manave śāśad=avratān tvachaṁ kṛishṇām=arandhayat* (I. 130.8), "Indra who in a hundred ways has preserved the Ārya worshipper......has subjected the dusky skin to the Manus." It is difficult to avoid the conclusion that the authors of the hymns believed themselves to be Āryas in race or stock and Manus in worship or religion. I hope I am not overshooting the mark if I say that originally the race which styled itself Ārya followed the Manu form of worship before

13. Most of these instances have been culled together in Muir's *Sanskrit Texts,* Vol. I, 162 and *ff.*

they penetrated India. Manu has survived in *Mānava* or *Mānusha* of Indian vernaculars and in 'man,' 'mann' and so forth of the English and other cognate European languages. But it has lost original signification and now denotes the human race.

But the Āryas were not non-proselytisers. Many members of the non-Āryan tribes or races espoused the Manu cult and were merged into the Ārya race. The tribes which followed the non-Manu worships were promiscuously designated Dāsa in the earlier period, although the term Dāsa, as has been pointed out above, originally denoted the Dahaē on the Caspian Steppes. In fact, so far as the Ṛig-Veda is concerned the Āryas have been contradistinguished from the Dāsas or Dasyus. In slightly later times Śūdra takes the place of Dāsa. Śūdra occurs only once in the Ṛig-Veda; that is, in the *Purusha-sūkta,* where however the meaning of the term is not explicit. Most probably it did not denote the fourth and last division of the Aryan community, as it did in later times. In viewing and studying the social life of the Ṛig-Vedic period, we can never be too much on our guard to see that we do not adopt the angle of vision of the later Dharmaśāstra. The Dharmasūtras and the Manusaṁhitā describe Śūdras as forming the well-known servile caste of the Aryan social structure. But was it so originally ? We cannot decide the point so far as the Rig-Veda goes, because Purusha-sūkta is the only hymn that makes mention of it. It is true that here the Śūdras are associated with the Brāhmaṇs, Rājanyas and Viśas and raise the presumption that the term Śūdra has been used here in the sense in which it occurs in the Dharmaśāstra. But we are in a better position in regard to the Atharva-Vēda. In this Veda, Śūdra stands in precisely the same contrast to Ārya that Dāsa or Dasyu does in the Ṛig-Veda. Thus Atharva-Vēda has ; *tay—āhaṁ sarvaṁ paśyāmi yaś=cha Śūdra ut=Āryaḥ*—(IV. 20.4), "With it (i.e. the herb) do I see every one, he who is Śūdra or he who is Ārya." The next text is: *ten=āhaṁ sarvaṁ paśyāmi uta Śūdram=ut=Āryam*—(*AV.,* IV. 20.8), "With him (i.e. the Yātudhāna) do I see everyone, whether Śūdra or Ārya." The third text runs thus : *priyaṁ mā kṛiṇu deveshu priyaṁ rājasu mā kṛiṇu priyaṁ sarvasya paśyata uta Śūdre ut=Ārye* (*AV.,* XIX. 62.1), "Make me thou dear to the gods, make me dear to kings, dear to every one that sees, whether Śūdra or Ārya." The fourth text is as follows : *priyaṁ mā darbha kṛiṇu brahma-rājanyābhyāṁ Śūdrāya ch=Āryāya cha* (XIX 32.8), "Make me, O *darbha,* dear to Brāhmaṇ and Rājanya, and to Śūdra and to Ārya."

The above extracts are enough to show that Śūdra is contrasted with Ārya in the Atharva-Veda as lucidly and vividly as Dāsa or Dasyu is with Ārya in the Ṛig-Veda. There can thus be no doubt that Śūdras denoted foreigners or aboriginals who were different from Āryas in stock and religion. But Dasyu or Dāsa, we have seen, originally denoted the Dahaë living about the Caspian Steppes. Is there any reason to suppose that Śūdra similarly denoted a tribe or a race ? Now, it is well-known that when the Macedonian emperor, Alexander, was conquering the north-west part of India he, on leaving the confluence of the Panjāb rivers, sailed down the Indus to the realm of a people called Sogdi by Arrian and Sodrāe by Diodorus. Sogdi has been identified by some scholars with the Soḍhās, a Rajput clan, and the Sodrāe with the Śūdras who thus "may be regarded" says McCrindle" as a remnant of the primitive stock which peopled the country before the advent of the Aryans."[14] It must be confessed that the variant Sogdi does not easily run into Soḍhā. On the other hand, Sodrāe can easily be identified with Śūdra. In that case, Sogdi can equally easily be recognised as a misreading for Sodrāe. The idea of Śūdra being the name of a tribe is no doubt a little curious. And some further evidence may be thought desirable in support of it. Attention may therefore be drawn to the fact that Sydroi has actually been mentioned by Ptolemy as one of the peoples inhabiting Northern Arachosia.[15] Further we may also note the compound word *Śūdr-Ābhīram* mentioned by Patañjali. On Pāṇini's *sūtra* I. 2.72, there is a *Vārtika* saying that no Dvandva compound is possible between two words one of which expresses 'generality' (*sāmānya*) and the other 'particularity' (*viśēsha*). In connection with this Vārtika Patañjali gives three examples, namely, *Śūdr-Ābhīram*, *gō-balīvardam*, and *triṇ-ōpalaṁ*. The *Vārtika* does not apply to any one of these instances, a critic may urge, because in every one of them, the first word expresses 'generality' and the second 'particularity.' To take the example with which we are concerned, namely, *Śūdr-Ābhīram*, the first word *Śūdra*, it may be contended, being a *sāmānya* is more extensive than and consequently includes, the *viśesha*, that is, Ābhīra. To this Patañjali gives the reply *Ābhīrā jāty-antarāṇi*, "Ābhīras are a tribe distinct from (Śūdras)." The conclusion is obvious that uptill Patañjali's time, Śūdras were as much a tribe as Ābhīras.

14. *Ancient India*, Vol. I, p. 354.
15. *I.A.*, Vol. XIII, p. 409.

But on what grounds does the critic think that Śūdra includes Ābhīra and consequently the compound *Śūdr-Ābhīram* is inadmissible ? In what sense does he take the word *Śūdra* ? Does he mean that Śūdra here denotes the lowest class of Aryan Society such as we understand at present, the degraded servile class from whom we cannot take water or food and for whom the Vedic *saṁskāras* are tabooed ? We ought not to interpret the social life of Patañjali's age from our present-day angle of vision. We had rather interpret it in the light of what Patañjali has said in another place in his *Mahābhāshya*. Elsewhere and not very long ago I had drawn the attention of scholars to a passage from the Mahābhāshya which comments upon Pāṇini's Sūtra : *Śūdrāṇām=aniravasitānām.*[16] In his gloss thereupon he enumerates a number of Śūdra groups which occupied different grades in the social scale prevalent in his time. Thus there were Chaṇḍālas and Mṛitapas, or, Ḍōmbas, as Kaiyyaṭa calls them, who, though they were in Āryāvarta, were excluded not only from sacrificial performance but from eating food from the plate of an Aryan. Similarly, there were Takshans and Āyaskaras—carpenters and blacksmiths, Rajakas and Tantuvāyas—washermen and weavers, who were no doubt debarred from the performance of a sacrifice but could eat from the Aryan dish without permanently defiling it. These Śūdras are well-known to us even to this day. But there are other Śūdras in the time of Patañjali who were outside Āryāvarta but who stayed in the same villages, hamlets, markets or towns with the Aryans. They, however, in virtue of their mental and ethical attainments imbibed the Ārya culture to such an extent that they were allowed to perform a sacrifice and could with impunity eat from the Aryan plate without making it permanently unclean. These Śūdras were Kishkindha and Gandhika, Śaka and Yavana, and Śaurya and Krauñcha. We know hardly anything about Kishkindha-Gandhika and Śaurya-Krauñcha. But we do know that the Śakas were Scythians and the Yavanas the Greeks, that, in other words, they were foreigners. In what sense then does the grammarian understand the term Śūdra ? Obviously he means by Śūdra anybody who is not a full-fledged Ārya, be he an outright barbarian or a foreigner who has partially but not fully imbibed the culture of the Āryas. In the present case, the Śakas and Yavanas had no doubt adopted the Aryan mode of worship and were therefore entitled to a certain degree of social dignity in the Aryan estimation. But apparently they had not adopted

16. *I.C.*, Vol. I, p. 275 *ff*.

the essential feature of Aryan Brahmanic culture, namely, the *Varṇ-Āśrama-dharma.* Therefore they were not full-fledged Āryas and had to be relegated to the class of Śūdras. That this is the sense in which Patañjali understands the term Śūdra is clear from the gloss of Nāgeśa on this passage. For says he: *Śūdra-śabdō=tra sūtre traivarṇik-ētara-paraḥ,* "In this Śūtra, the word Śūdra denotes a person other than a member of the three *varṇas*;" that is to say, Śūdra is one who is not a Brāhmaṇ, who is not a Kshatriya and who is not a Vaiśya and denotes every other body from the whole world. This is just the point we have to remember regarding Śūdra. Śūdra like Dāsa certainly denoted originally a tribe, but afterwards came to signify anybody who was not a full-fledged Ārya. He may be a veritable barbarian or aboriginal. He may be a foreigner endowed with culture. He may be even such a foreigner as has partially assimilated Arya culture. But if he has not imbibed this culture fully and wholly, especially in its social aspect, he *is* a Śūdra.

LECTURE II

ARYAN CULTURE

In this Lecture we shall set ourselves to the task of ascertaining what Aryan culture was. This is, however, a task beset with great difficulties. The earliest productions of this culture are the four Vedas, the Brāhmaṇas, and the Upanishads. But none of these compositions aims at describing the socio-religious structure of the Aryan community. This has been set forth only in the Dharma-sūtras and the Arthaśāstra. Unfortunately these works are of a late period. In fact, none of them is much earlier than the fourth century B.C. Our only duty in these circumstances is in the first instance to find out what they say about the Aryan social structure and to ascertain thereafter how far the information so gleaned is corroborated by the incidental references to its various features contained in the Vedic literature. In this manner alone can we decide what the Aryan culture originally was and what accretions it received in course of time.

Now, this subject has been clearly and succinctly treated by Kauṭalya in his Arthaśāstra, in Chapter III of Book I. "The three Vedas, namely Sāman, Ṛik and Yajus," says he, "constitute Trayī, (that is, the Veda-Trinity). The well-known Law of Trayī is serviceable inasmuch as it settles the specific duties of the four Varṇas and the four Āśramas." Kauṭalya then proceeds to specify the duties of the four Varṇas, which, according to him, are the Brāhmaṇ, Kshatriya, Vaiśya and Śūdra. Thereupon he speaks of the Aśramas, and curiously enough he begins not with Bramachārin but with Gṛihastha. Any way the Āśramas he enumerates are the same, namely, Gṛihastha, Brahmachārin, Vānaprastha and Parivrājaka. He also specifies the duties obligatory upon each one of these Āśramas. But what good is it to perform the duties laid down for a Varṇa or an Āśrama? "(The observance of) one's own duty," replies Kauṭalya, "leads to (the attainment of) heaven and infinite bliss (*ānantya*). If it is transgressed, the world is snapped through confusion (*saṁkara*)." In support of this statement, Kauṭalya quotes two verses which may be rendered as follows: "Hence the king shall not allow the people to swerve from their own duty. For he who performs his own duty rejoices here and hereafter. With the Ārya rules of conduct established, with Varṇa and Āśrama stabilised (and) being indeed protected by Trayī, the world progresses, never perishes." This was certainly the view which prevailed in the fourth century B.C., and is also that maintained by Dharmaśāstra. How far was it prevalent in the time of the Ṛig-Veda ? This is the question that now arises and that we have now to tackle.

Let us first take the question of Varṇa. Kauṭalya and the authorities on the Dharmaśāstra divide Aryan society into the four Varṇas: Brāhmaṇ, Kshatriya, Vaiśya and Śūdra. But did these Varṇas exist in the time of the Ṛig-Veda ? I have already drawn attention to the Purusha-sūkta (*RV.*, X. 90.12) which says with reference to Purusha : " The Brāhmaṇ was his mouth, the Rājanya was made his arms ; the being (called) the Vaiśya, was his thighs ; the Śūdra sprang from his feet." It is true that here the Brāhmaṇ, Rājanya, Vaiśya and Śūdra have been mentioned in consecutive order, corresponding to Brāhman, Kshatriya, Vaiśya and Śūdra of the Law books. But we have already seen that the term Śūdra of this hymn cannot mean exactly the same thing as Śūdra of the later period. At any rate, Śūdra did not form an integral part of the Aryan community in the Ṛigvedic times but denoted barbarians or foreigners who were not full-fledged Aryans socially and religiously. In fact, the Śūdras have been differentiated from the Āryas in the Atharva-vēda just as the Dasyus or Dāsas have been from them in the Ṛig-Veda. Why then, it may be asked, Śūdras have been mentioned at all in the Purusha-sūkta ? The reply is a simple one. Ṛik 2 of this hymn says : " Purusha himself is this whole (universe), whatever has been and whatever shall be." Mankind forms one part of this universe, and consequently it was divided into the four sections : the Brāhmaṇs, Rājanyas and Vaiśyas who constituted the Aryan world and the Śūdras, the fourth section, which denoted the rest of mankind. It is not simply the mouth, arms, thighs and feet of this Purusha that have been so allegorically treated. There are other parts of his body which have been similarly described. Thus the moon sprang from his mind (*manas*), the sun from his eye, Vāyu from his breath, and so forth and so on. It will thus be seen that there is nothing to show that the Śūdras constituted an integral division of the Aryan society when the Ṛig-Veda was being composed. In fact, even at the risk of repetition, we may point out that the Brāhmaṇs, Rājanyas and Vaiśyas formed the normal sections of the Aryan community and that the Śūdras signified the non-Aryan part of mankind. If any further proof is needed in support of this inference, it is furnished by the first quarters of three Ṛiks, namely,

Brahma jinvatam=uta jinvataṁ dhiyo........Kshatraṁ jinvatam=uta jinvataṁ nṛīn....dhenūr=jinvatam=uta jinvataṁ Viśo ......(*RV.*, VIII. 35. 16-18) "Strengthen the Brāhmaṇs, animate (their) thoughts (O Aśvins!)......strengthen the Kshatras, strengthen (their) men of war......strengthen the milch-kine, strengthen the Viśas......" It will be seen that these Ṛiks speak of Brahma, Kshatra and Viśas only. As no Śūdras are here mentioned, the conclusion is irresistible that they are not mentioned because they did not then form any integral part of the Aryan society. This agrees with the inference that Śūdras are referred to in the Purusha-sūkta because they had to describe the whole of mankind, the Brāhmaṇs, Rājanyas and Viśas forming the Aryan, and the Śūdras the non-Aryan, section of mankind. In fact, the meaning of the word Śūdra had not settled down even in the time of Patañjali, as we have also pointed out in the last Lecture. It denoted anybody who was not a Brāhmaṇ, who was not a Kshatriya, who was not a Vaiśya. A foreigner even with strong proclivities towards Aryan culture was relegated to the Śūdra class if he was not a full-fledged Aryan.

Though the Aryan society was in the Ṛigvedic epoch divided into the three sections just mentioned, they could not have been more than mere classes,—they could have hardly crystallised into castes. We have evidence of some members of the Rājanya class not only being authors of hymns but also exercising priestly functions. Thus we have a Ṛishi named Paruchchhepa whom the Anukramaṇī credits with the composition of Ṛig-Veda I. 127-39 and designates Daivōdāsi, i.e., son of Divōdāsa, who was doubtless a Rājanya. Or we may take the case of Dēvāpi Ārshṭishēṇa who and his brother Śantanu were princes of the Kuru tribe. The elder was Dēvāpi, but Śantanu got himself anointed king, whereupon there was no rain in his kingdom for twelve years. The drought being attributed by the Brāhmaṇs to his having superseded his elder brother, Śantanu offered the kingdom to Dēvāpi. The latter, however, refused it, but acting as Purōhita, or, family priest, for his brother sung a hymn of his own composition, namely, Ṛig-Veda X. 98, dispelled the drought and brought back the rains. This story has been narrated by Yāska in the Nirukta,[1] who is a fairly early authority. Or, again, we may take the case of Viśvāmitra, a Ṛishi, to whom the Third Maṇḍala of the Ṛig-Veda has been attributed. The Pañchaviṁśa Brāhmaṇa[2] calls him a king and a

1. II, 10.

2. XXI, 12, 2.

descendant of Jahnu, and the Aitarēya Brāhmaṇa supports the statement. Nay, it is confirmed by Ṛig-Veda III. 43, a hymn standing to the credit of Viśvāmitra himself and setting forth his personal history. Ṛik 5 of this hymn is: *Kuvin=mā-gopāṁ karase janasya kuvid=rājānaṁ Maghavann=ṛijī shin Kuvid ma=ṛishiṁ papivāṁsaṁ sutasya kuvin=me vasvo amṛitasya śikshāḥ,* "Wilt thou not make me guardian (*gōpa*) of the people, make me their king (*rājan*), O impetuous Maghavan, make me a Ṛishi that has drunk of Soma ? Wilt thou not give me imperishable wealth?" This means that the author of this hymn, who could be no other than Viśvāmitra, was not only a ruler and king but also a Ṛishi through the grace of Maghavan (Indra). In fact, though there was this division of the Aryans into three classes based upon difference of occupation, there was not yet any absolute separation of the functions of these classes. The inference is supported by Ṛig-Veda IX. 112.3 which runs thus: *Kārur=ahaṁ tato bhishag=upala-prakshiṇi nanā nānā-dhiyō vasūyavō=nu gā iva tasthima Indrāy=Ēndo parisrava,* "A bard am I, my father a physician, my mother a grinder (of corn) on stones. With varied plans, striving for wealth, we run after (our respective objects) like kine. Flow, Indu, for Indra's sake." As there was thus no fine demarcation of castes based upon various callings, the idea of *varṇa-saṁkara* or confusion of castes referred to by Kauṭalya and Dharmaśāstras and ever present to the Indian mind thereafter could not possibly have arisen in the Ṛigvedic period.

Let us now see how far the idea of Āśrama had developed in the Ṛigvedic epoch. The term Āśrama was not known before the Upanishadic period. In fact, its earliest use as denoting the stages of a Hindu's life is found in the Śvētāśvatara Upanishad.[3] It is therefore no wonder if the Āśramas are not mentioned as such in the Ṛig-Veda. Nevertheless, the institutions of the student (*brahmachārin*), the householder (*gṛihapati*) and the Muni are already there. Thus the use of the term Brahmachārin is found in Ṛig-Veda, X. 109.5. There Bṛihaspati has been represented as separated from his wife and wandering about like a Brahmachārin. The word here has doubtless been used in the secondary sense of 'celibacy, continence.' This itself presupposes the primary sense of the term, namely, 'a religious student solely devoted to the study of the Vedas.' Even the teaching of a hymn by a teacher to his pupils is referred in Ṛig-Veda VII. 103, the celebrated Frog hymn,

3 VI. 21.

the author of which is of course Vasishṭha Ṛishi. Ṛik 5 has: *Yad=ēshām=anyō anyasya vācham śāktasy=ēva vadati śikshamāṇaḥ | sarvaṁ tad=ēshāṁ samṛidh=ēva parva yat suvāchō vadathan =ādhy=apsu,* "When of these one repeats the utterance of the other just as a learner utters that of the teacher, your every limb seems to be growing larger as ye prate with eloquence on the waters." In this Ṛik the poet, moved by the awakening of the frogs at the beginning of the rainy season, compares their croaking with the clamour of pupils reciting the Vedic *mantras* in imitation of their teacher. The Brahmachārin has been praised in the Atharva-Veda[4] also which prescribes for him practically the same duties as in the Dharmaśāstras. The householder, gṛihapa or gṛihapati, is mentioned repeatedly in the hymns, as well as in later Vedic works. To take one instance, Ṛig-Veda VI. 53.2 has: *abhi no naryaṁ vasu vīraṁ prayata-dakshiṇaṁ | vāmam gṛiha-patiṁ naya,* "Take us to the wealth that men require, the manly master of a house, free-handed with the liberal mind." What the Ṛishi in this Ṛik evidently means is that he desires the god Pūshan to take him to a householder who will institute sacrifices and liberally reward the officiating priests. In regard to the two institutions just described, attention may be drawn to the Taittirīya-saṁhitā,[5] which says: "A Brāhmaṇ on birth is born with a threefold debt, of pupilship (*brahmacharya*) to the Ṛishis, of sacrifices to the gods, of offspring to the Pitṛis. He is freed from his debt who has a son (*putrī*), is a sacrificer (*yajvā*) and has lived as a pupil (*brahmachārin*)."[6] Here the term Brahmachārin occurs also in this Saṁhitā, and the words *putrī* and *yajvā* mentioned in this passage obviously refer to the Gṛihastha stage of life though it has not been verbally mentioned.

The next point of our enquiry is whether the third and fourth life-stages are at all referred to in the Saṁhitā. Ṛig-Veda X. 136 describes the Muni, also called the Kēśin, 'the long-haired one.' Though he wears garments soiled and of yellow hue, he is wind-clad at the girdle, that is, naked in the middle.[7] Impelled by the gods (*dēv-ēshita*) and transported with the ecstasy of a Muni (*un-māditāḥ maunēyēna*) he pursues the winds, flies through the air, perceiving all forms, dwells in both the oceans, the eastern and the

4. XI. 5, 1 *ff*.
5. VI. 3, 10, 5.
6. *Harvard Ori. Series*, Vol. 19, p. 526.
7. This shows probably the influence of the Vrātya cult described in Lecture IV.

western, treading the path of sylvan beasts, celestial nymphs and minstrels, and so forth and so on. What the hymn means is that by the dint of *Maunēya unmāda* the Muni can attain to the fellowship of the deities of the air, the Vāyus, the Rudras, the Apsarases, and the Gandharvas, and, endowed like them with miraculous powers, can travel along with them in their course. Transcending even this, the Muni, or 'the long-haired one',[8] so called because he cannot shave his hair during the time of his austerities, upholds fire, moisture, heaven, and earth and resembles the world of light. There is also another class of ascetics metioned in the Ṛig-Veda[9] in connection with the Bhṛigus who were also credited with occult powers: *Yad=dēvā yatayo yathā bhuvanēny=apinvata* (*RV.*, X. 72.7), "when, O ye gods, like Yatis, ye caused all existing things to grow." That there was a difference between Munis and Yatis in the Saṁhitā is clear from many references. Thus, while Ṛig-Vēda VIII. 17.14 says: *Indro munīnāṁ sakhā,* "Indra is the Friend of Munis," there are many passages from the Samhitās which describes this god as killing the Yatis. Thus the Taittirīya-saṁhitā (VI. 2, 7.5) has: "Indra gave the Yatis to the Sālāvṛikas; them they ate on the right of the high altar... "; and in the same breath we are further told that "they overcame the Asuras, their foes." The same thing is repeated in the Aitarēya-Brāhmaṇa (VII. 28), which says: "(Indra) cast down Vṛitra, threw Yatis before *sālāvṛikas........*" The Pañchaviṁśa-Brāhmaṇa (XIV. 4.7), contains a story, saying that Indra restored to life Vaikhānasas who had been killed by the Asuras at a place called Muni-maraṇa. This shows that Vaikhānasas were apparently the same as the Munis and that the Yatis[10] probably belonged to the Asura community who did not worship Indra. It thus seems that the Munis at least belonged to the Manu cult and the Aryan community, and that as they wore a tattered garment and long hair on their body, and subjected themselves to austerities, they were what in later times were called Vānaprasthas. Although Brahmachārins, Gṛihapas or Gṛihapatis and Munis are referred to in the Ṛig-Vēda, there is nothing to show that the institutions were inter-related. Of course, this system of life-stages developed in the Upanishads and was in full operation in the Śūtra period. Thus the Baudhāyana-Dharmasūtra (II. 10 17.15) says: *āśramād=āśramam=upanīya brahma-pūtrō bhavat=īti vijñāyatē,* "Entering order after order,

8. Compare also *RV.*, VII. 56, 8.
9. VIII. 3, 9; 6, 18.
10. *V.O.J.*, Vol. XXIII. pp. 9-17.

man is known to become one with Brahman." Nevertheless, it must be admitted that even in the Sūtra period there was a great difference of opinion re. the Āśrama one should embrace, and consequently there was not perfect unanimity in regard to the super-excellence of any one of these orders. Thus Gautama begins Chapter III, with the words *tasy=āśrama-vikalpam=ēkē bruvatē,* "some lay down option re. the order one should enter upon." And the very next but one Sūtra reads: *tēshāṁ gṛihasthō yōnir=aprajanatvād=itarēshām,* "the householder is the source of these, because the others do not produce offspring." After giving a description of the four orders, Gautama concludes: *aikāśramyaṁ tv=āchāryāḥ pratyaksha-vidhānād=gārhasthaya gārhasthasya,* "But the teachers prescribe one order only, because the order of the householders is explicitly prescribed (in the Vedas)." Haradatta in his gloss upon this passage makes the following remarks: "The duties of householder, the Agnihōtra and the like, are frequently prescribed and praised in all the Vedas, Dharmaśāstras, and Itihāsas. As, therefore, the order of householders is explicitly prescribed, this alone is the order (obligatory on all men). But the other orders are prescribed only for those unfit for the duties of a householder. That is the opinion of many teachers."

The object of this Lecture is to ascertain what Aryan culture originally was. In coming to a decision on this point we have to take our stand, as far as possible, on the Saṁhitās in general and the Ṛig-Vēda-saṁhitā in particular. We have also pointed out that about the middle of the fourth century B. C. Ārya *dharma* was supposed to be based on *varṇ-āśrama.* We know what these Varṇas and Āśramas ordinarily denote. We have further shown that so far as the first three Varṇas are concerned, they were prevalent in the Ṛigvedic period. They certainly did not crystallise into impervious castes such as they are at present or even such as they were when the Manu-saṁhitā was compiled. We have to guard ourselves against viewing the Ṛigvedic period with Manu's eyes or interpreting the Ṛigvedic life from the mediæval point of view. Nothing could be more unhistoric. Nothing could be more untrue. In regard to the Varṇas, we find that they were mere classes so that an Aryan could at will change one for the other. In fact, this sort of things prevailed uptil the Gupta period, though about the commencement of the Christian era the hardening process had already begun, as we shall see later on. It is not our object to trace the rise and development of Ṛigvedic Varṇas into modern castes. Nor is it our object to see how the Āśramas or stages of life emerged and evolved themselves into a progressive inter-related order. Both the topics are of a most fascinating character, but demand another series of Lectures for their lucid and effective treatment. Our object here is simply to discuss what exactly the Aryan culture was when the Aryans penetrated India along with allied tribes. One feature of this culture and civilisation was the division of mankind into four sections: Brāhmaṇs, Rājanyas and Viśes who then constituted the Aryan society, together with the Śūdras who denoted the rest of mankind consisting of the non-Aryans. Another feature was the existence of the three institutions of the Brahmachārin, Gṛihapati and Muni which corresponded to the three of the later Āśramas: Brahmachārin, Gṛihastha and Vānaprastha. Along with the Gṛihastha *āśrama* are associated a number of *saṁskāras* or sacraments. Whether and how many of them were in existence in the time of the Ṛig-Vēda is not certain. But one point about this Aryan culture which is noteworthy is the fanaticism which the sacerdotal classes displayed in the dissemination of their ritualistic religion, or the *Vratas* as they called them. This point has already been dwelt upon in the last Lecture, where many Ṛiks were cited in support of it. Another but a new passage may be cited in this connection: *akarmā Dasyur=abhi no amantur=anya-vratō amānushaḥ* | *tvaṁ tasy=āmitrahan vadhar=dāsasya dambhaya* (*RV.*, X. 22.8), "Around us is the Dasyu, without rites, void of sense, with different rites, not following Manu. Baffle, thou Slayer of the foe, the weapon which this Dāsa yields." The pretext for the contempt of these Dasyus that is dinned into our ears is that they did not observe the Aryan rites. In the Ṛig-Veda, they are often taunted as "men without worship" "men without rites" and so on. The Aryans, especially the sacerdotal classes, with all the arrogance and narrowness of fanatics never thought that there could be any other rites except their own. This fanatical character of the Aryan priests subsisted for a long time, till in fact, the worship of the Vedic gods lasted. They did not even brook the idea of an Aryan going to any part of India which had not been completely Brahmanised. To cite a later instance, the Baudhāyana-dharmasūtra (I. 1.14) says: "He who has visited the (countries of the) Āraṭṭas, Kāraskaras Puṇḍras, Sauvīras, Vaṅgas, Kaliṅgas, (or) Prānūnas shall offer a Punastōma or a Sarvapṛishṭha (*ishṭi*)." There can be no doubt that some of the Aryans of Vedic period were of an aggressively proselytising character and spread their culture and civilisation through conquest. We will dilate on this point in the next Lecture. Nevertheless, it cannot possibly be denied that causes of a pacific and truly religious nature were also in operation in the dissemination of this culture. There was something unique also in the ethical and religious speculations of the Ṛigvedic Aryans which held the human soul spell-bound. It is true that the general impression created on our mind by the study of the Ṛig-Veda is the domination of the priestly class saturated with selfish sordid aims. This is noticeable particularly in their prayers. Thus Ṛig-Veda VI. 12·6 *Veshi rāyō vi yāsi duchchhuna madema śata-himāḥ suvīrāḥ*, "Bring wealth, drive away affliction. May we enjoy ourselves for a hundred winters with brave sons!" In this wise the Vedic hymns pray for wealth, food, drink, wines, children, long life and every conceivable object of pleasure and comfort. Nevertheless, side by side with them are some bright rays of sunshine in this gloom and darkness of earthiness and worldliness. Thus Ṛig-Veda X. 7·3 says: "I deem Agni (my) Father, Kinsman, Brother (and) Friend for ever." Or take Ṛig-Veda X. 22·3 "Indra holds the fearless thunderbolt as a father would for his dear son." This shows that the Vedic Aryans approached gods with a remarkable familiarity, yet with a solemn regard, after the manner of the most advanced conception of modern times. If this is the case, it is no wonder if some of the hymns were strongly tinctured with henotheism or the exaltation of one single god at a time, as was first pointed out by Max Müller. Thus Ṛig-Veda I. 101.3 has: "Of Indra, whose great might is heaven and earth, in whose law abide Varuṇa and Sūrya, whose law the rivers follow as they flow—we invoke him with the Maruts to become our friend." Or we may take the case of Varuna, who influence, the scholars say, was waning in the Ṛigvedic period. Thus sings one Ṛigvedic poet (I. 25. 7-11): "Varuṇa knows the way of the birds that fly in the air. He knows the way of the ships on the sea. True to Law, he knows the twelve months with their progeny (=the days). He knows also that which is born · alongside of them (the intercalary month). He knows the track of the spreading, high, and mighty winds. He knows (the gods) that sit upon them. The Strong One, true to Law, sits down on his seat to rule over all. From thence he marks and sees all his wondrous works, that have been, and that are to be." I am afraid, it is impossible even for the Bible to surpass this description of the omnipresent, omnipotent and omniscient Varuṇa. The question here arises: how did this henotheism at all arise—this exaltation of one single god for the time being and to the exclusion of others? The answer is that the idea of the supreme soul must have already dawned upon the Ṛigvedic mind which afterwards dominated the whole Indian philosophy. Thus in Ṛig-Veda X. 121 Prajāpati has been praised not only as the creator and preserver of the world, but also as *yo deveshv=adhi deva eka āsīt*, that is, as ' (one) who has been *the one* god above the gods.' Nay, in verse after verse of this hymn recurs the refrain *kasmai devāya havishā vidhema* " to what god shall we offer our oblation," wherein lies hidden the thought that there is no other deity than Prajāpati in the whole plurality of the gods to whom the oblation can be offered. When once the idea of Supreme Soul sprung up, it is but natural that all other gods should be looked upon as his manifestations. The well-known Ṛik bearing upon this point is: *Indraṁ Mitraṁ Varuṇam=Agnim=āhur=atho divyaḥ sa Suparṇo Garutmān| ekaṁ sad=viprā bahudhā vadanty= Agniṁ Yamaṁ Mātariśvānaṁ=āhuḥ* || (*RV.*, I. 164.46). "They call him Indra, Mitra, Varuṇa, Agni, and that celestial noble-winged Garutman. Sages name variously that which is but one; they call it Agni, Yama and Mātariśvan." This is the grandest Ṛik I have lighted upon in the whole range of the Ṛigvedic hymns, whose syncretising potency is infinite. When we turn to the popular cults which bulk so large in modern Hinduism, it is argued, they are so amazingly unlike anything we can label Aryan. " A student of the Hinduism of the masses," they say, " is certain to be struck by (1) the veneration of the cow, (2) the popularity of Gaṇēśa and (3) the ubiquitous appearance of the bull and the snake." " Is there a hint," they ask, " of any one of them in a context incontestably Aryan ? " " They fit the ideas of the Indianisation of the Aryans more readily than anything we can call the Aryanisation of India "—so they conclude. It is, however, forgotten that all the seemingly incoherent elements of the work-a-day Hinduism have been held together simply on account of the sublime notion *ekaṁ sad=viprā bahudhā vadanti*, ' Sages name variously that which is but one '—a notion which has permeated all masses. With the advent of the present century I was for some time a serious student of religion in Poona. Consequently I came in contact with many Christian missionaries of repute. With one of them I had once a serious discussion on the idol and fetish worship embedded in Hinduism. I maintained that no Hindu believed in an idol or fetish as God,—a proposition to which my missionary friend took strong exception. Determined to put the matter to the test, we set out of his house—" A pair of Friends, though I was young, And Matthew seventy-two." We repaired to what was then the loveliest spot of Poona—the Modi Baugh. Not far from it was a fountain which broke from the turf " and gurgled at our feet." There we saw a man worshipping something on the brink of the brook. As soon as his worship was over, the missionary was the first to accost and address him in Marāṭhī. "What god were you worshipping here? Here I see nothing but a rough uncouth piece of stone bedaubed with redlead"—interrogated the missionary. "I was worshipping the god Khaṇḍōba," was the rejoinder. "What prayer of yours can this hideous stone hear? And what can this Khaṇḍōba grant you?" "It is not exactly the stone that I was worshipping. I was worshipping really the Supreme Deity of whom this stone is a symbol and this Khaṇḍōba, Masōbā or any other god is a mere manifestation" retorted the Hindu worshipper. The missionary received the pertinent reply, and our controversy ended. To come back to our point, the idea involved in *ekaṁ sad=viprā bahudhā vadanti* has fused all the jarring faiths of India into Hinduism which at rock bottom is thus faith in one universal god. This is the priceless legacy which India has received from Aryan culture and which has unified all opposite and contradictory faiths and cults into that mysterious Hinduism.

There may however be some philosophers here who may contend that these Ṛigvedic speculations about religion are all right so far as they go, but contain no ethical elements. But is it so really? Those who have studied the hymns addressed to Varuṇa know full well that the attributes and functions ascribed to this god impart to his character a moral elevation and sanctity far surpassing that ascribed to any other Ṛigvedic deity. Thus Ṛig-Veda VII. 86.3-6 has the following: "I ask myself, Varuṇa, what my sin was, and try to find it out. I go to ask those who know. One answer only the wise men give me: 'It is Varuṇa that is angry with thee.' What great offence is it, Varuṇa, for which thou seekest to slay thy worshipper and friend? Tell me, O mighty and glorious One. Then shall I, freed from sin, come speedily to thee with adoration. Do thou disentangle us from the sins of (our) fathers (and) from those which we have committed in our own persons. Do thou disentangle Vasishṭha, O king, as a robber is who has stolen cattle, or as a calf is from its tether." But what were the trying circumstances that had occasioned these sins? The poet replies: "It was not our will, Varuṇa, but some seduction which led us astray—wine, anger, dice or thoughtlessness; (also) the stronger perverts the weaker. Even sleep removeth not all evil." It is this verse which imparts to the hymn a human touch of an exceedingly fine character. Even the holy Vasishṭha cannot lay his hand to his breast and say that he is above all temptation and thoughtlessness, above the seduction of wine and dice!! There are many other verses from the Ṛig-Veda which are of sublime import and which will ravish the mind of even the present age. Time however forbids our considering and appreciating them. But I cannot resist the temptation of quoting one of them here. It is thus: *Dvā suparṇā sayujā sakhāyā samānaṁ vṛigshaṁ parishvajāte tayōr=anyaḥ pippalaṁ svādv=atty=anaśnann =anyō=bhichākaśīti.* This occurs in Ṛig-Veda I. 164.20 and is adopted verbatim in Muṇḍaka (III. 1.1) and Śvētāśvatara Upanishad (IV. 6). In both the Upanishads it is associated with another verse which makes the sense whole and entire. We are therefore compelled to take them both together and translate them as follows: "Two Birds, inseparables and friends, cling to the same tree. One of them eats the sweet fruit, the other observes without eating." "On the same tree sits man grieving, immersed, bewildered by his own impotence. But his grief passes away when he sees the other one, supreme, contended, and knows his glory." It is impossible to light upon any passages in the whole of the Sanskrit literature which poetically, yet succinctly, describe the interrelation of the Individual, and the Supreme, Soul.

Let us now pause and digest. It cannot be denied that there must have been something in the spectacular side of the Ṛigvedic culture. These were the celebration of sacrifices, performance of sacraments, the socio-religious order consisting of what later came to be known as Varṇa and Āśrama, which could attract any barbarians or foreigners of the Ṛigvedic period. When to these is added the fanaticism of the priests, it can scarcely be doubted that the externals of religion not only produced a fairly deep impression upon the non-Aryans of that epoch but also secured a fair number of converts, who were held together in a close grip by the members of the sacerdotal classes. But man is not content with things as they are but looks for something beyond. "There is an Infinite in him," says Carlyle, "which with all his cunning he cannot quite bury under the Finite. Will the whole Finance Ministers and Upholsterers and Confectioners of modern Europe undertake in joint-stock company, to make one Shoeblack happy? He cannot accomplish it, above an hour or two; for the Shoeblack also has a Soul quite other than his Stomach; and would require, if you consider it, for his permanent satisfaction and saturation, simply this allotment, no more, and no less: *God's infinite Universe altogether to himself,* therein to enjoy infinitely, and fill every wish as fast as it rose." The ceremonial demonstrations and the paraphernalia of the Ṛigvedic priest must have doubtless impressed the non-Aryan mind, but the effect could not have been a permanent one. On the other hand, the religious and ethical speculations of the Ṛigvedic poet-seers were as varied as they were unique. We have just seen that the Individual and the Supreme Soul have been described as inseparables and friends, perched on the top of the tree, namely, the universe. We have seen in what terms of tender sweet relationship some Aryans of the Ṛigvedic age have addressed the gods, calling them 'father, brother and friend.' We have also seen that there are pretty frequent prayers for deliverance from sin, the conception of which is considered to be a sure index of the religious depth of a race or community. They are the hymns addressed mostly to Varuṇa which bear a close analogy to the devotional psalms of the Bible both in point of language and ideas—passages which are rare to be met with in the literature of the Upanishads. They also had conception of life after death in which they firmly believed. The Ṛig-Veda comprises speculations also of a philosophical character, such as those comprised in hymns X. 5, 27, 88, and 129. I do not quite understand why so much encomium is lavished upon the Upanishads and why so little on these hymns of the Ṛig-Veda. If the Upanishads are a product of dry reason and thought, the Ṛig-Veda is a hymnology replete with emotion and imagination of a high order. If the former appealed to the microscopic minority, the latter must surely have appealed to the macrocosmic majority, of the foreigners and barbarians with whom the Aryans came into contact in India. What Hellenism was to Asia Minor, Syria, Iran and Babylonia, Aryanism, i.e., the Aryan Culture, proved itself to India and Greater India.

LECTURE III

ARYANISATION

In this Lecture we shall discuss some points connected with the dissemination of the Aryan culture, or the Aryanisation as it may be called. The term 'Aryanisation' is resented in some quarters. Why not say instead 'Indianisation of Aryan Culture' —they ask. As a matter of fact, both the views are correct. Different tribes and races entered India at different times, bringing their own culture in their wake. There were the Aryans, the Asuras or Assyrians, the Greeks, the Scythians, the Ābhīras, the Gurjaras, the Moghuls, and, last but not least, the English, with their western culture which is perhaps the most virile of all cultures ever introduced in this country. These different races and tribes have impressed at different times their thoughts and emotions, tastes and tendencies upon the people of India, and the national genius has manifested itself in the process of absorption, in the judicious selection and harmonious blending of those features which are permanent and humane. When again a new civilisation comes into impact with an old one, it produces a stunning effect if it is of a superior and more virile character. Such was the case when the Greek culture came in contact with the Roman. Such is the case with the Western Culture which the British have brought to India. "Cato the elder," says Carlyle in one place, "used to tell them (the Romans), 'the instant you get the Greek literature among you there will be an end of the old Roman spirit.' He was not listened to; the rage for Greek speculation increased; he himself found it impossible to keep back, although he grew very angry about it, and in his old age he learned the Greek language and had it taught to his sons. It was too late; nobody could believe any longer, and every one had set his mind on being a man and thinking for himself." Similarly, when India came in contact with the British culture, such cataclystic changes were taking place that there was a time when educated India was completely anglicised. Although a century or more has elapsed since the contact of these two cultures, it is doubtful whether the real Indianisation of the British culture has commenced.

Such was exactly the case when there was an impact of the Aryan and non-Aryan cultures in India three milleniums of years ago. The effect of it is perceptible to this day. In the last Lecture we have discussed how the sublime notion involved in *ekaṁ sad=viprā bahudhā vadanti* has syncretised all opposite and contradictory cults and beliefs into that mysterious religion called Hinduism which, at rock bottom, as I have already remarked, is faith in one universal soul. Another permanent effect produced by Aryan culture is the development of what has been called Sanskritic languages. We cannot do better than quote the following opinion of Sir George Grierson, an eminent linguist of the day. " When an Aryan tongue," says he, " comes into contact with an uncivilized aboriginal one, it is invariably the latter which goes to the wall. The Aryan does not attempt to speak it, and the necessities of intercourse compelled the aborigine to use a broken 'pigeon' form of the language of a superior civilisation. As generations pass, this mixed jargon more and more approximates to its model, and in process of time the old aboriginal language is forgotten and dies a natural death."[1] We may whole-heartedly endorse this view of Sir George Grierson except in one respect. This exception is the Dravidian languages which are the vernaculars of South India. We do not know how the Aryan, failed to supplant the Dravidian, speech, in this part of India, though it most thoroughly did in Northern India, where, no doubt, the Dravidian tongue prevailed along with the Muṇḍā before the advent of the Aryans. It is well-known that " Brahuī, the language of the mountaineers in the Khanship of Kelat in Beluchistan, contains not only some Dravidian words, but a considerable infusion of distinctively Dravidian forms and idioms."[2] The discovery of this Dravidian element in a language spoken beyond the Indus tends to show that the tribes, who originally spoke the Dravidian language, must have, like the Aryans, the Scythians and so on, entered India by the north-western route. This also explains why the Ṛigvedic language has borrowed words from the Dravidian and has also its phonetics affected by the Dravidian. Nevertheless, this much is certain that when the Aryans once penetrated India and established themselves there, their speech supplanted the Dravidian as far south as, and including, Mahārāshṭra. Whether the English tongue will ever succeed in establishing similar derivative vernaculars all over India we do not know. But this much is certain that the Aryans achieved such a complete cultural victory over India that its effect is perceptible to this day in the shape

1. *Imperial Gazetteer of India*, Vol. I, pp. 351-52.
2. Caldwell, *Grammar of the Dravidian Languages*, Intro., pp. 43-44.

of the Sanskritic languages that are prevalent over two-thirds of this country. It must, however, be admitted that the domination, even for centuries, of the Aryan culture over South India was somehow not enough for the eradication of the Dravidian languages.

It is, no doubt, curious that the Dravidian, should be supplanted by the Aryan, language in North India, but not in South India, although Aryan civilisation had permeated South India as much as North India. And what is more curious is that on the other side of the Madras Presidency, that is, Ceylon, the indegenous language was superseded by the Aryan tongue with the spread of Aryan culture. It should not however be thought that even in the Dravidian part of the country no Aryan tongue was ever spoken or understood by the natives after the Aryans came and were settled there. The earliest inscriptions that have been deciphered and understood are those of Aśoka. Three sets of his Minor Rock Edicts have been found in the Chitaldrug District of Mysore. Another set of the same Edicts along with one set of his Fourteen Rock Edicts has been discovered at Yerraguḍi in the Kurnool District of the Madras Presidency. They are all couched in the court language of Magadha modified by the local dialects. His object in inscribing his edicts was that people should know what Dhaṁma was and practise it and that the neighbouring monarchs and his own descendants should tread in his footsteps with a view to disseminate Dhaṁma.[3] There was no meaning in Aśoka engraving his edicts in the Chitaldrug and Kurnool Districts of South India if the people of those parts could not understand the language thereof, which was anything but Dravidian. But the language of the Aśoka inscriptions soon gave way to a language which is called Monumental Prākṛit and which bears the closest affinity to the Pāli of the Southern Buddhist Scriptures. It seems to be the parent of the Prākṛit which in later times came to be known as Mahārāshṭrī. Perhaps it was this province which supplied its dialect to meet the new demand,—how we do not know at present. And what was originally a provincial dialect began to rise to the eminence of a universal language, and became the Hindustānī of Ancient India from c. 200 B.C. to c. 450 A.D. It became not only the official or political language of the country, but also the language of the scriptures and religious benefactions. Thus the royal charters issued by Gautamīputra Sātakarni and Vāsishṭhīputra Puḷumāvi of the Śātavāhana dynasty,

3. D. R. Bhandarkar's *Aśoka*, p. 153 *ff*., and 290.

the Vaishṇava inscription on the Besnagar Pillar of the Yavana or Greek ambassador Heliodorus, and even the Nānāghṭ Cave epigraph of Sātakarṇi, in spite of the fact that it describes his numerous Brahmanical sacrifices, have all been couched in the Monumental Prākṛit. Nay, the scriptures of the Buddhists which seem originally to have been composed in the Māgadhī were now recast in this Hindustānī of Ancient India, afterwards known as Pāli. When exactly this all-India language sprang into existence is not known. It may not be in the reign of Aśoka, but certainly during the Mauryan supremacy, and as a result of their imperial rule. And further we have incontestable evidence that upto the fourth century A.D. the Monumental Prākṛit was the official language of the kings even in those provinces where Dravidian languages are now supreme. At least one stone inscription and five copper-plate characters have been found in these provinces, ranging from the second to the fourth or fifth century A.D. The stone inscription was found at Maḷavaḷḷi in Shimogā District, Mysore State.[4] It registers some grant to the god Maḷapaḷi by Viṇhukaḍa Chuṭukalānaṁda Sātakarṇi of the Kadamba dynasty who calls himself king of Vaijayantī and records the renewal of the same grant by his son. Vaijayantī, we know, is Banavāsī in the North Canara District, Bombay Presidency. At Banavāsī, too, we have found an inscription of the queen of this king. Both Banavāsī and Maḷavaḷḷi are situated in the Canarese-speaking country, and yet we find that the official language here is the Monumental Prākṛit. The same conclusion is proved with reference to the Tāmiḷ-speaking country by the five copper-plate grants referred to above. Of these five three belong to the Pallava dynasty reigning at Kāñchīpura, one to a king called Jayavarman of the Bṛihatphalāyana *gōtra*, and one to the Sāḷaṅkāyana Vijayadēvavarman. The fact that every one of these is a title-deed and has been drawn up in Monumental Prākṛit shows that this Aryan language, at least upto the fourth century A.D., was spoken and understood by all classes of people in a country of which the capital was Kāñchīpura and which was and is now a centre of the Tāmiḷ language and literature.

The question that now arises is: what was the state of things when the Aryans conquered parts of India and the Aryan culture began to spread over the whole country. The reply is that what happened in India with the introduction of English culture must

4. *Carmichael Lectures*, 1918, p. 32 *ff*.

have happened also in this country when the Aryan culture impinged upon the non-Aryan. If we take Bengal into consideration for the time being, it is well-known that the Bengalis, possessed as they are of poetic emotion and artistic imagination, took to writing poetry, not in Bengali but in English. Michael Madhu Sudan Dutt, the greatest native poet of Bengal in the 19th century, began his career by writing English verses in 1848 when he was in Madras, though later on he won literary distinction by writing in his own language. What, again, about Miss Toru Dutt? So far as we know, she wrote nothing in Bengali, but in French and English. Her best work in English is *Ancient Ballads and Legends of Hindustan;* and of these poems *Our Casuarina Tree,* they say, is rich in imagery and musical cadences. Above all, what about Mrs. Sarojini Naidu, who is one of the greatest nationalists of Modern India? She is also recognised to be a poetess of great eminence. But all her poems, so far as we know, are in English. If such is the case with Modern India, what wonder is there if the non-Aryan peoples of Ancient India adopted Vedic Sanskrit as the vehicle of expression for their thought and emotion? This conclusion is forced upon us by a critical study of the Atharva-Veda.

It is well-known that wherever, in old works, there is mention of sacred knowledge, there the Trayī comprising Ṛig-Veda, Yajur-Veda and Sāma-Veda only is mentioned; the Atharva-Veda always follows it and sometimes is completely ignored. Why does the Atharva-Veda occupy a comparatively low position? In this connection Bal Gangadhar Tilak[5] draws our attention to the views of the French savant, Lenormant, who has justly observed that while the Aryans worshipped the good and beneficent deities in nature, the Mongolians, to which race the Chaldeans belonged, always tried to propitiate the malevolent spirits; hence while sacrifice formed the main feature of the Vedic religion, magic and sorcery was the main characteristic of the religion of the ancient Chaldeans. Not that there were no Chaldean hymns, but even these were used for magic purposes. Tilak has drawn our attention in this connection to one passage from the Atharva-Veda (V.13), which is a hymn against snake poison.

5. *Chaldean and Indian Vedas,* p. 32 ff. (published in R. G. Bhandarkar Commemoration Volume).

Asitasya *Taimātasya* babhror=apodakasya cha|
sātrāsāhasy=āhaṁ manyor=ava jyām=iva dhanvano vi muñchāmi rathāṁ iva || 6
Āligī cha *Viligī* cha pitā cha mātā cha|
Vidma vaḥ sarvato bandv=arasāḥ kiṁ karishayatha || 7
Urugūlāyā duhitā jātā dāsy=asiknyāḥ|
pratankaṁ dadrushīṇāṁ sarvāsām=arasaṁ visham || 8

(V. 6)—I release (thee) from the fury of the altogether powerful Taimāta, of the black, the brown, or the waterless, (serpent); as the bow-string (is loosened) from the bow, as chariots (from the horses).

(V. 7)—Āligī and Viligī are (your) father and mother. We know (your) kin completely. Deprived of (your) strength, what will you do ?

(V. 8)—The daughter of Urugūlā, the slave, born of the black one,—of all those who have run to their hiding place, the poison is bereft of force.

Now, this passage bristles with such foreign terms that no previous translator could throw any light, whether Bloomfield, Griffith or Whitney. Like the Nairuktas they were content with suggesting tentative derivations. No Aitihāsika or historian came forward for a long time to interpret the Atharva-Veda. It was Tilak who was the pioneer in this matter. It is true that the word Taimāta occurs again in Atharva-Veda V. 18.4, but "the serpent Taimāta," says he, "is, I am sure, no other than the primeval water dragon Tiāmat generally represented as a female but sometimes even a male monster snake in the Chaldean cosmogonic legends........Tiāmat is the well-known Chaldean androgynous dragon whose fight with Marduk is the subject of some of the Cuneiform tablets of the creation legends." Marduk and Tiāmat are to the Chaldean, what Indra and Ahi are to the Vedic, Pantheon. "As regards *Urugūlā*," says Tilak, "the word appears as *Urugala* or *Urugula* in the Accadian language. Literally it means 'the great (*gal=gula*) city (*uru*),' but is generally used to denote the great nether world, the abode of the dead—a place visited by Istar in her search for her lover Dumuzi or Tamuz. Personified, it means the deity of the nether world, and a female snake can be fitly described as Uru-gula's daughter." Tilak, however, was not able to trace Āligī and Viligī. Neverthless, he rightly points out that they "appear to be Accadian words, for there is an Assyrian god called *Bil* and *Bil-gi*."

There are many other words of foreign origin which are found also in the Ṛig-Veda. One of these is *apsu* which forms part of such compound words as Apsujit (VIII. 13.2; IX. 106.3) and Apsu-khit (I. 139.11) which are other names of Indra and which signify 'the conqueror of Apsu.' There are Nairuktas and Nairuktas (philologists and philologists) who will explain the phrase by treating its first member, namely, *apsu,* as a locative of *ap* water and joining it with *jit* or *kshit* and making an *aluk-samāsa* of the whole. But this is a forced construction. It is more natural and simpler to take the first member as the Chaldean word *Apsu* or *Abzu,* represented as the husband of Tiāmat and denoting the primaeval chaos or watery abyss. The main features of the Tiāmat-Marduk struggle are also to be found in the Ahi (=Vṛitra) -Indra fight described in the Ṛig-Veda. It is because Indra released the waters enveloped and hemmed in by Ahi (=Vṛitra), the Vedic Tiāmat, that the former has been styled, Apsu-jit. Nay, there is a much closer resemblance between the legends about the Vedic Indra and the Chaldean Marduk. There is the sevenfold division of the earth's continents by the Babylonians which corresponds to the sevenfold division found not only in the Purāṇas but also in the Vedas. Nay, "the serpent Tiāmat killed by Marduk is sometimes represented as having seven heads, while Indra is called *Sapta-han* or the "Killer of Seven" in the Vedas (*RV*. X. 49.8), and the closed watery ocean, the doors of which Indra and Agni opened by their prowess, is described as *sapta-budhna* (seven-bottomed) in *RV*. VIII. 40.5."

When two civilisations came into contact with each other, it is natural to expect some borrowing on both sides. But Indra is Indra, and Marduk is Marduk, whatever the few points of resemblance may be; so that we can safely say that, after all, Indra is a Ṛigvedic deity. The same thing we cannot say in regard to Taimāta, Āligī, Viligī and Urugūla which are out and out Chaldean godlings and which, as we have to note, are mentioned in the Atharva-Veda only. That does not mean that words of foreign origin are not found at all in the Ṛig-Veda. We have already referred to the word *Apsu.* We may now refer to the word *Yahva* and its cognates *Yahu, Yahvat, Yahvī* and *Yahvatī* which occur in the Ṛig-Veda. We may compare it to the Chaldean *Yahve* from which the Biblical secret name of God, *Jehovah,* has been derived. But perhaps the most important word of foreign origin which is found in the Ṛig-Veda is Asura. As a rule, this term has been used in a good sense in this hymnology, not only with reference to Varuṇa, Mitra-Varuṇa, Rudra, Pūshan, Marut, Soma and Savitṛi but also with reference to Indra. That this word bore a good sense is clear from Ṛig-Veda VII. 65.2 where Mitra-Varuṇa have been described *tā hi devānām=asurā,* "they are the Asuras of gods," that is, "the most supreme of all deities." Nevertheless, the term occurs also in a bad sense, though in a few instances only. Thus the gods, we are told, smote the Asuras (X. 157.4). Similarly, Agni promises to utter a hymn by which the gods may vanquish their foemen the Asuras (X. 53.4). And the epithet *Asurahan,* 'Asura-slayer' is found applied to Indra (VI. 22.4), Agni (VII. 13.1), and the Sun (X. 170.2). Nay, in one place (VIII. 85.9), Indra is invoked to scatter 'the godless Asuras.' The phrase 'the godless Asuras' shows that Asura was the name of a people or tribe. This agrees with the fact that Bṛihaspati is besought to pierce with a bolt the heroes of an Asura called Vṛikadvaras (II. 30.4). In one place (X. 138.3), Indra, associating himself with Ṛijishvan, is represented to have overthrown the forts of Pipru, the conjuring Asura. Similarly, Indra-Vishṇu smote down a hundred times a thousand heroes of a third Asura named Varchin (VII. 99.5). It will thus be seen that Asura has been used in two senses, namely, (1) 'the supreme deity' and (2) a people named Asura. Who could these Asuras be? I have elsewhere pointed out that they were the Assyrians, amongst whom also the term Assur was used in these two senses, as is clear from Cuneiform Inscriptions.[6] Nay, these Asuras or Assyrians seem to have carved kingdoms in India also. How else can we explain Bṛihaspati having killed the heroes of Asura Vṛikadvaras and Indra having destroyed the forts of Asura Pipru? Vṛikadvaras and Pipru must have been Asura kings ruling over some parts of India. Further, I have already drawn attention to Ṛig-Veda VIII. 85.9 where Asuras are called 'godless.' Let me quote the whole verse here: *Tigmam=āyudhaṁ Marutām=anīkaṁ kas=ta Indra prati vajraṁ dadharsha | anāyudhāso asurā adevāś=chakreṇa tāṁ apa vapa Ṛijīshin,* "A sharpened weapon is the host of Maruts. Who, Indra, dares withstand thy bolt of thunder? Weaponless are the godless Asuras: scatter them with thy discus, Impetuous Hero." The phrase *adevā Asurāḥ* 'the godless Asuras' reminds us of *avratā Dasyavaḥ* 'the riteless Dasyus' and leads us to the inference that, like the Dasyus, the Asuras were different from the Āryas not only in race but also in religion. That these Asuras again were somehow connected with Chaldaea may be seen from the fact that there are at least two Ṛiks where they

6. D. R. Bhandarkar's *Aśoka,* p. 225 *ff.*

are credited with *māyā* or magical powers. Thus Ṛig-Veda X. 124.5 is: *nirmāyā u tye Asura abhūvan=tvaṁ cha mā Varuṇa kāmayāse| ṛitena rājann=anṛitaṁ viviñchan mama rāshṭrasy=ādhipatyam=ēhi,* "These Asuras have lost their powers of magic. Be thou, O Varuṇa, if thou dost love me, O King, discerning truth and right from falsehood, come and be Lord and Ruler of my kingdom." Similarly Ṛig-Veda X. 138.3, to which we have already referred, has *dṛihḷāni Pipro=Asurasya māyino Indro vy=āsyach =chakṛivāṁ Ṛijiśvanā,* "In alliance with Ṛijiśvan Indra shattered the solid forts of Pipru, possessed of *māyā* (magical powers)." It is difficult to avoid the conclusion that these Asuras were Assurs or Assyrians who were settled down in the different parts of India and possessed kingdoms of their own and were credited with magical powers which constituted the essence of the Chaldean cult. As they were thus of divergent stock and religion, it is natural that the Āryas should condemn them as 'godless' and invoke the assistance of their gods to overthrow their kings and their power. What then becomes of the Ṛiks in which the Ṛigvedic deities Varuṇa, Mitra-Varuṇa, Rudra, Pūshan, Marut, Soma, Savitṛi and Indra have been called Asura and, above all, in one of which Mitra-Varuṇa have been styled *devānām=Asurā,* 'the Asura or most supreme of deities'? These Ṛiks are found not only in the later Maṇḍalas I and X but also in the earlier Maṇḍalas, such as II., V., VII. and VIII. The conclusion is almost irresistible that the hymns in question were composed by those Asuras who had embraced the Aryan faith especially when we take into consideration the fact that some of these extol Agni and Indra. They are, *par excellence,* Aryan Ṛigvedic gods, who never spared any hostile clans of divergent faith and who, with special reference to this trait in their character, have actually been called *Asurahan.* This alone can explain why in some hymns they are styled Asura and why in some *Asurahan.* The latter certainly must have been composed by poets who were antagonistic to Asura in race and faith. If this position is accepted, we have also to conclude that the other hymns where they are called Asura were composed by poets who, though they perhaps continued to pertain to the Asura stock, yet were converts to the Aryan faith. Enmity between the Aryans and Assyrians increased in the post-Ṛigvedic period. Even as early as the Atharva-Veda Asura means 'demon' only. And in the Brāhmaṇas the Asuras are associated with darkness. Nevertheless their human character was not forgotten. In fact, one section of this Asura race has been called Prāchya, in the Śatapatha-Brāhmaṇa, who not only spoke a Mlechchha language but had their own Brāhmaṇs or priests.[7] And Prāchya, we know, was another name for Magadha or South Behār. According to the Purāṇas and the Mahābhārata, Aṅga, Vaṅga, Puṇḍra, Suhma and Kaliṅga were called after the princes of these names who were the five sons of the Asura king Bali. The whole of East India, comprising these provinces, was therefore designated *Bālēya-kshētra* and had their own priests also called Bālēya Brāhmaṇs.[8] Even as late as the seventh century A.D., Bhāskaravarman, king of Prāgjyōtishapura and contemporary and ally of Harshavardhana of Kanauj, traced his descent from Narakāsura. Two centuries later we have two royal families ruling over Assam who were similarly descended from the Asuras Naraka and Bhagadatta of epic fame. But that the Asuras are demons or imaginary beings is so much impressed on our mind by the post-Vedic literature that we cannot conceive of any Asuras to be a living people now. Nevertheless it is worthy of note that the Asuras are still living as a non-Aryan tribe[9] in Chhotā-Nagpur in Behār, just in that Prāchya country which was in the time of the Śatapatha-Brāhmana occupied by the Asuras.

There is however no trace of the Asuras who espoused the Aryan faith in the Ṛigvedic period and worshipped the Vedic deities. They have by now been so completely merged into the Indian population that it does not survive even in a surname. The Baudhāyana-śrautasūtra[10] however has preserved it in the name Āsurāyaṇa, a branch of the Kaśyapa *gōtra*. One of their customs had been preserved for a long time in the Āsura mode of marriage mentioned by the Dharmasūtras. Thus the Āpastambīya-Dharmasūtra (II. 5.12.1), has *śakti-vishayēṇa dravyāṇi dattvā vahēran=sa Āsuraḥ*, "If they marry after paying a price (for the bride), that is the Āsura (form)." Bride-price was the order of the day among the Assyrians and the Babylonians, the difference being that amongst the former it was paid to the woman and among the latter to her father.[11] The custom of the bride purchase has been referred to even in Ṛig-Veda I. 109.2: *aśravaṁ hi bhūridāvattarā vijāmātur=uta vā ghā syālāt*, "For I have heard that ye give wealth more freely than a disreputable son-in-law does (to

7. *S.B.E.*, Vol. XLIX, pp. 423-24; XII, p. 29.

8. *An. Bhand. Ori. Res. Inst.*, Vol. XII, p. 114 *ff*.

9. *Ency. Rel. Eth.*, Vol. II, pp. 157-59. Also, *J.B.O.R.S.*, Vol. III, pp. 567 & *ff*.; Vol. XII, pp. 147 & *ff*.

10. (Bibliotheca Indica Edition), Vol. III, p. 450.

11. *Encyclopaedia Britannica*, Vol. II, pp. 863-64. See also Prof. A. S. Altekar's *Position of Women in Hindu Civilisation*, pp. 46-47.

his future father-in-law)." But the case is entirely different in regard to the cult centering round Taimāta, Ālīgī, Valigī and Urugūla and furnishing a magic formula. The Atharva-Veda bristles with spells and incantations, belonging both to holy and black magic, which were repugnant to the Vedic Aryan mind. How many of them were Chaldean and how many non-Aryan Indian it is difficult to say. This much, however, is certain that they were antagonistic to the Manu cult of the Vedic Aryans, and consequently belonged to the Chaldean and non-Aryan wizard-priests. And yet these magic formulæ are couched, not in a foreign language, but in Vedic Sanskrit! What can it mean? It can only mean that when the Vedic Aryan culture began to dominate India, Vedic Sanskrit became the vehicle of expression which was used by various exotic cults of the period to serve their end. This much however is indisputable that when foreign magical incantations and formulæ were introduced into Vedic Sanskrit literature, it was natural that the work now called Atharva-Veda, which contained these incantations, should come to be looked upon with scant respect and even with contempt by the Vedic community. This explains why it was excluded from the canon of sacred texts. And, in fact, it was not called Atharva-Veda before the Sūtra period, its old name being *Atharvāṅgirasaḥ*, that is, "the Atharvans and the Aṅgirases." Nevertheless, it cannot be denied that beside the adoption of the Vedic Sanskrit as a vehicle of expression, this ancient magic poetry shows signs of brahmanisation. A whole group of hymns of the Atharva-Veda is concerned with the interests of the Brāhmaṇs, the feeding of priests, the fees for the sacrifice and so forth. But it does not necessarily follow from it that the Brāhmaṇs here referred to pertained to the Vedic Aryan religion. Just as the Asuras or Assyrians of the Śatapatha-Brāhmaṇas had their own Brāhmaṇs, the followers of the Chaldean cult of the Atharva-Veda may have their own Brāhmaṇs, who were in reality magic priests. Similiarly, here also we meet with the same gods as in the Ṛig-Veda, such as Indra, Agni and so on; but their original character has quite faded. "They hardly differ from each other," says Winternitz,[12] "their original signification as natural beings is, for the greater part, forgotten; and as the magic songs deal mostly with the banishment and destruction of demons the gods being invoked for this purpose—they have all become demon-killers." This is the Chaldeanisation of the Aryan culture, and reminds us of the remark of the French scholar,

12. *A History of Indian Literature*, Vol. I, p. 124.

Lenormant, cited above. "Not that there were no Chaldean hymns to the sun-god, but even these were used for magic purposes." Such seems to have been the case even with the Chaldean priests settled in India. One typical instance may be adduced. Atharva-Veda IV. 16 contains the following magnificent hymn to Varuṇa, the first half of which describes the omnipotence and omniscience of the god in language familiar to us from the Ṛig-Veda and the Psalms, but the second half is nothing but a vigorous exorcism-formula against liars and libellers. I repeat the first half in the poetical rendering of Muir:[13]

> "The mighty Lord on high our deeds, as if at hand, espies;
> The gods know all men do, though men would fain their acts disguise [1]
>
> Whoever stands, whoever moves, or steals from place to place,
> Or hides him in his secret cell,—the gods his movements trace.
> Wherever two together plot, and deem they are alone,
> King Varuṇa is there, a third, and all their schemes are known. [2]
>
> This earth is his, to him belong those vast and boundless skies;
> Both seas within him rest, and yet in that small pool he lies. [3]
>
> Whoever far beyond the sky should think his way to wing.
> He could not there elude the grasp of Varuṇa the king.
> His spies, descending from the skies, glide all this world around;
> Their thousand eyes all-scanning sweep to earth's remotest bound. [4]
>
> Whate'er exists in heaven and earth, whatever beyond the skies,
> Before the eyes of Varuṇa, the king, unfolded lies.
> The ceaseless winkings all he counts of every mortal's eyes,
> He wields this universal frame as gamester throws his dice." [5]

13. *Original Sanskrit Texts*, etc., Vol. V, p. 64, n. 126.

All this is genuinely emotional, devotional and poetic. But now we see how the hymn suddenly changes and ends. Here I read the prose translation given by Bloomfield.[14]

> " May all thy fateful toils which, seven by seven threefold, lie spread out, ensnare him that speaks falsehood: him that speaks the truth they shall let go! [6]
>
> With a hundred snares, O Varuṇa, surround him, let the liar not go free from thee, O thou that observest men! The rogue shall sit his belly hanging loose, like a cask without hoops, bursting all about! [7]
>
> With (the snare of) Varuṇa which is fastened lengthwise and that which (is fastened) broadwise, with the indigenous and the foreign, with the divine and the human, [8]
>
> With all these snares do I fetter thee, O.N.N., descended from N. N., the son of the woman N. N.: all these do I design for thee." [9]

In regard to this hymn Roth makes the following pertinent remarks: " There is no other song in the whole of Vedic literature, which expresses the divine omniscience in such impressive words, and yet this beautiful work of art has been degraded into the exordium of an exorcism. Still, here as with many other portions of this Veda, we may surmise that available fragments of older hymns were used for the purpose of re-furbishing magic formulæ. As a fragment of this kind the first five or even six verses of our hymn may be considered ".[15] We entirely agree. Surely Chaldeanisation of Aryan culture cannot further go, and it looks that this hymn was composed for the benefit of an Asura convert to Aryan faith who could not however steer clear of his old superstition and belief in witchcraft.

14. *S.B.E.*, Vol. XLII, p. 88 *f.*
15. *Abhandlung über den Atharvaveda*, Tübingen, 1856, p. 29 *f.*

LECTURE IV

ARYANISATION (*continued*)

Our account of the impact of Aryan culture upon the non-Aryan peoples and their religious beliefs cannot be complete unless we critically consider who the Vrātyas were. According to the Pañchaviṁśa-Brāhmaṇa, there were four kinds of Vrātyas. One of these is the *Hīnas* or the Libidinous Class who deteriorate by staying in Vrāti settlement and who neither practise *Brahmacharya* nor pursue agriculture or trade (XVII. 1.2). They are Kanishṭhas (XVII. 3.2). They are further distinguished into the two classes: Arhants 'saints' and Yaudhas 'warriors' corresponding to the Brāhmaṇ and Kshatriya grades of the Aryan community. Another class was known as the *Garagir* or Swallowers of Poison to whom commoners' victuals taste like Brāhmaṇ's food (XVII, 1.9), who, though not consecrated, speak the tongue of the consecrated and yet call what is easy of utterance difficult to utter. A third class was represented apparently by men designated *Śama-nīchā-mēḍhra* (XVII. 4. 1) "those whose *mēḍhra* hangs low through control of (sexual ?) passion." They are Jyēshṭhas. They also reside in the Vrāti settlement. Some details are also forthcoming of the life and dress of the Vrātyas. Their Gṛihapati or leader wore an *ushṇīsha* or turban which he put on one side of the head. He carried a *pratōda* or whip and a *jyāhrōḍa* or some special kind of bow and drove in a *vipatha* or rough wagon covered with planks and wore a silver neck ornament called *nishka*. He was clad in a black garment and two *ajinas* or skins, one black and one white. The garment of those subordinate to Gṛihapati have also been specified, but we need not trouble ourselves with those details.[1]

But the earliest description of the Vrātya is furnished by Atharva-Veda, Book XV. A Vrātya there was, we are told, just going about. He stirred up Prajāpati who in turn saw in himself gold and generated that. That gold in the course of

1. For a general description of the Vrātyas, see Rajaram Ramkrishna Bhagavat's *A Chapter from the Tāṇḍya Brāhmaṇa of the Sāma Veda*, &c., &c., *J.B.B.R.A.S.*, Vol. XIX, pp. 357 & *ff*; and Macdonell and Keith's *Vedic Index*, &c., Vol. II. pp. 342 & *ff*. For Nishka see also *Carmichael Lectures*, 1921, pp. 66 *ff*.

evolution became *brahman*. Vrātya waxed great and became Mahādēva. He further compassed the lordship of the gods and became Īśāna. He became Ēka-Vrātya. He took to himself a bow; that was Indra's bow. He moved out towards the eastern quarter. After him moved out both the *bṛihat* and *rathaṁtara* and the Ādityas and all the gods .... Of him in the eastern quarter, *śraddhā* or faith is the *puṁśchalī* or harlot; Mitra is the Māgadha;......day, the *ushṇīsha* or turban,......yellow, the *pravartas* or ear-rings, *kalmalī*, the *maṇi* or jewel........mind, the *vipatha* or rough vehicle, Mātariśvan and Pavamāna, the two horses of the rough vehicle; the wind, the charioteer; the whirlwind, the *pratōda* or whip. Similarly, he moves out towards the southern, western and northern quarter, and his appurtenances similarly change. A sort of asceticism also we find associated with him. Thus Atharva-Veda XV.1.3 connects him with *tapas*. In XV.3.1, we are told that he stood erect for a whole year, and in XV.15.1-2 that he had seven *prāṇas* (breaths), seven *apānas* (expirations) and seven *vyānas* (out-breathings).

This book of the Atharva-Veda obviously sets forth the mystic glorification of the Vrātya who seems to be the deity of some non-Aryan cult regarded differently by his original votary now that he has imbibed the Aryan culture in full. All the appurtenances that pertained to the god previously have been explained metaphorically to suit the recent conversion. Thus what was originally his *puṁśchalī* or harlot has now become *śraddhā*. What was originally his Māgadha or priest has become the Vedic god Mitra, and so forth and so on. After the god Vrātya his worshippers also were known as Vrātya. That this was a non-Aryan cult can scarcely be doubted. How else can we explain the specification of such appendage as *puṁśchalī*, Māgadha, *ushṇīsha, pravartas, vipatha* and so forth which are nowhere found associated with any Vedic Aryan deity? Nay, we have seen above that they speak the same language as those who have been consecrated but nevertheless call what is easily spoken hard to pronounce. This clearly shows that they were some non-Aryan people who had adopted the Aryan tongue but were not yet masters of the same. Their social structure also points to the same inference. They had no Vaiśya class, because we are distinctly told that they neither tilled the land nor did any business. And the two classes they had were known, not as Brāhmaṇ and Kshatriya, but as Arhant and Yōdha, who carried on depredations. If any doubt still remains on this point, it is removed by the fact that Vrātya, Puṁśchalī and Māgadha are included in the list of victims at the Purushamēdha or human sacrifice in the Yajur-Veda.[2] Here, of course, the Vrātya denotes not the deity, but the worshipper of that deity. And as he and Māgadha have been looked upon as fit victims for Purushamēdha, they must naturally have belonged to a sect whose tenets were particularly repugnant to the Aryan mind. But do we know anything, it may now be asked about the nature of these tenets? Atharva-Veda, Book XV, Sec. 5, it is worthy of note, speaks of Bhava, Śarva, Paśupati, Ugra, Rudra, Mahādēva and Īśāna in ascending order as becoming the attendants of Ēka-Vrātya, as he moved out in the various intermediate directions. This means that they were originally looked upon as the manifestations of Ēka-Vrātya.[3] It is not unreasonable to infer that the original Śiva sect was known as Vrātya. It had several characteristic features which it shared with Śivism of the later period. Thus Ēka-Vrātya is represented to have taken to himself a bow that was Indra's bow (XV. 1.6), to have been fond of the strong drink *surā* (XV. 9.2), to wear *ushṇīsha* or turban and to be attended upon by the *puṁśchalī* or harlot and by Māgadha (XV. 2.1-4). What Māgadha most probably denotes we shall see later on. But it is here sufficient to note that Śiva of the post-Vedic period was noted for a formidable bow, was fond of *surā* and of dancing *tāṇḍava* along with drunken imps, and wore *ushṇīsha* and was therefore called *ushṇīshin.* It will thus be seen that the *Vrātya-sūkta* of the Atharva-Veda is the mystic description of Ēka-Vrātya, the original Śiva deity, given by a votary who was previously a rank follower of that sect but who was afterwards so steeped in Aryan culture that he sublimated the Vrātya cult just as the modern worshippers of Kṛishṇa explain away metaphorically the god's dalliances with the Gōpīs.

Our knowledge of the earliest form of Śiva worship cannot be complete unless we supplement the above account with what we can elicit from other sections of the Vedic literature. But the earliest representations of this worship are found in the seals, terracotta figurines and so forth exhumed by Sir John Marshall from different sites in the Indus Valley and described in his classical work " Mohenjo-daro and the Indus Civilisation." The god shown on the seal illustrated in Plate XII.17 is doubtless a prototype of the historic Śiva, because he is three-faced, seated in an attitude of *Yōga* and with *ūrdhva-mēḍhra* clearly exhibited. Crowning his head is

2. *Vājasanēya-saṁhitā,* XXX, 8.

3. The views set forth in this and the following paras have already been briefly expressed by me in *Jour. Ind. Soc. Ori. Art,* June-Dec. 1937, pp. 74 & *ff*.

a pair of horns meeting in a tall head-dress. This must be the *ushṇīsha,* which, as we have seen, has been mentioned in the Atharva-Veda. To either side of the god are four animals, an elephant, tiger, rhinoceros, and buffalo. This exhibits the aspect of the god as Paśupati. But his main characteristic is that he is three-faced. Śiva or Rudra is nowhere called *tri-mukha.* He is rather styled *try-ambaka,* which, though in post-Vedic literature, it means 'the three-eyed one,' must have borne a different signification in the Saṁhitā period. Thus Ṛig-Veda VII. 59.12 has: *Try-ambakaṁ yajāmahe sugandhiṁ pushṭivardhanam,* "Tryambaka we worship, sweet augmentor of prosperity." The Vājasaneya-saṁhitā (III. 58) has: *Esha te Rudra bhāgaḥ saha svasrā Ambikayā tañ juhasva svāhā | Esha te Rudra bhāgaḥ ākhus=te paśuḥ || Ava Rudram=adīmahy=ava devaṁ Tryambakam,* "This is thy portion, Rudra, graciously accept it together with thy sister Ambikā! Svāhā! This is thy portion; thy victim is mouse. We have satisfied Rudra; we have satisfied the god Tryambaka." On this text the Śatapatha-Brāhmaṇa (II.6.2.9) makes the following comment: *Ambikā hi vai nāma asya svasā|tay-āsya esha saha bhāgaḥ|tad=yad=yasya esha striyā saha bhāgas=tasmāt Tryambako nāma,* "Ambikā, indeed, is the name of his sister; and this share belongs to him along with her; since this share belongs to him with a *strī* or female, he is called Tryambaka." This philological explanation, however, of the name Tryambaka is anything but critical. For if this be accepted as the correct etymological derivation, we should have had the word, not even *stryambaka* but rather *stryambika.* As a matter of fact, it is Tryambaka. The natural explanation of the word has to be sought for elsewhere. One Vedic word meaning 'a mother' is *ambā* or *ambikā.* Thus in Ṛig-Veda II.41.16 Sarasvatī has been addressed not only as Ambā 'mother' but also Ambitamā 'the best of mothers'. Tryambaka must therefore mean '(the god) born of three mothers.' The case is not unlike the later Kārtikēya who was looked upon as a son of Śiva in the Paurāṇik period. Śiva, we are told, cast his seed into Agni, who, being unable to bear it, cast it into the Ganges. It was then transferred to the six Kṛittikās (when they had gone to bathe in the Ganges), each one of whom conceived and brought forth a son. These six sons were afterwards mysteriously combined into one of extraordinary form with six heads, twelve hands and twelve eyes. Hence he was called not only Kārtikēya but also Shaḍānana. A similar mysterious birth must have been attributed to Rudra who was for that reason called Tryambaka. He was thus three gods rolled into one, originally born of three different *ambikās* or mothers. And it is not impossible to distinguish between these three Ambās from among the figurines of Mother-Goddess found in the north-west of India. Some of them bear placid, and, some, grotesque faces. Some again are with children in their arms. Be that as it may, it is not impossible in this wise to detect these three types of Ambā from among the heaps of female figurines exhumed at Mohenjo-daro so as to account for Rudra being called Tryambaka and further to account for the three-faced divinity figuring on the seal of Mohenjo-daro. It is possible also to detect a fourth type, namely, that of a standing and almost nude female, elaborately dressed, profusely ornamented or both. They are apparently figures of the dancing girl. One such bronze statuette has been actually so recognised (Pl. XCIV.6-8). Can there be any doubt that they represent the *puṁśchalī* associated with Ēka-Vrātya ? We have not, however, considered the most important feature of the image portrayed on the Mohenjo-daro seal. It is worthy of note that whereas the upper part of his body is well clad and well ornamented. " the lower limbs are bare and the *ūrdhva-mēḍhra* clearly exhibited. "But it is possible," says Sir John Marshall, " that what appears to be the phallus is in reality the end of the waistband". This is what he says on page 52 of Vol. I. of his *Mohenjo-daro and the Indus Civilisation.* But in note 5 on page 55 he adds as has been correctly pointed out by Prof. Nilakanta Sastri,[4] " On the other hand, it is noteworthy that this is the manner in which Śiva's manifestation, Lakulīśa, is habitually portrayed" and refers to my paper on the subject published in *An. Rep., A. S. I.* 1906-07, p. 186, and figs. 2 and 5. And curiously enough, wherever I have lighted upon an icon of Lakulīśa, there his *ūrdhva-mēḍhra* has been clearly shown, and, as a matter of fact, the *Viśvakarm-āvatāra-Vāstu-śāstra* insists upon this as one of the three essential features of Lakulīśa. This is but natural. Further, as Śiva is never worshipped except in the form of the *linga*, Lakulīśa, though an incarnation of Śiva, cannot become an object of worship, unless his figure is conjoined to that of a *liṅga*. In fact, this is just what we see in the case of the two images of Lakulīśa which are at Kārvāṇ or Kāyāvarōhaṇa, the birth-place of this god, and which are worshipped by the people there. Secondly, what we have to note about these images is that Lakulīśa figures here in stark nudity. Two questions here arise : (1) how come these Śaiva images to be nude ? and (2) is there any evidence in support of Śiva, Rudra or Vrātya being represented with *ūrdhva-mēḍhra* ? In reply to the first question, attention may be drawn to

4. *The Cultural Heritage of India,* Vol. II, p. 22, *n.* 2.

two modern Śaiva sects, Kaṛā Liṅgīs and the Nāgās. In regard to the first of these Wilson says: "they go naked, and to mark their triumph over sensual desires, affix an iron ring and chain on the male organ; they are professedly worshippers of Śiva".[5] In regard to the Nāgas, the same authority tells us that "the Śaiva Sannyāsīs who go naked are distinguised by this term."[6] Attention in this connection may further be drawn to the Liṅga of the Paraśurām-ēśvara temple at Guḍimallam in the North Arcot District, Madras. There also the *liṅga* and the human figure are shown conjointly[7] in the sculpture which is of the fifth or sixth century A.D. The *liṅga* is represented in a rather ithyphallic style, but the figure in front is clad with a lower garment and in such a fashion as to show, through, the male organ which is here shown hanging down like that of the Tīrthaṁkara of the Digambara Jain sect and which reminds us of the phrase *śama-nīchā-mēḍhra* in the Pañchaviṁśā-Brāhmaṇa quoted above. This has been explained in the *Lāṭyāyana-śrauta-sūtra* by *sthāvirād=apēta-prajananā ye te śama-nīchā-mēḍhrā* (VIII.6.4), "*Śama-nīchā-mēḍhra* are those who through old age have lost the power of procreation." It is however, very doubtful whether this explanation is founded upon fact, because it is well-nigh impossible to single out those men who have through age lost their power of procreation. And further it is exceedingly singular and insulting to bring such people under one class and dub them *Śama-nīchā-mēḍhra*. The natural explanation would be to take that the Vrātyas divided themselves into two main classes, (1) those who worshipped their nude god with the male organ hanging down (*nīchā-mēḍhra*) as in the case of the Guḍimallam icon and (2) those whose god was portrayed with his organ upraised (*ūrdhva-mēḍhra*) as in the case of Lakulīśa. The first were noted for their *śama* or restraint of passion and styled Jyēshṭhas and the second, having no such ideal in view, were designated the *hīna* or libidinous class and also Kanishṭha. The Mohenjo-daro seal on which the god is represented as *ūrdhva-mēḍhra* must therefore be taken as denoting the second type of Śiva worship. This last must have been the prototype of the later Vāmāchārīs whose "worship is mostly celebrated in a mixed society, the men of which represent *Bhairavas* or *Vīras*, and the women *Bhairavī* or *Nāyikās*. The Śakti is personated by a naked female "and the ceremony is terminated with the most scandalous

5. *Essays on the Religion of the Hindus*, Vol. I, pp. 236-37.
6. *Ibid.*, p. 238.
7. *I.A.*, Vol. XL, p. 104. See also *Memoirs, A.S.I.*, No. 40, p. 24.

orgies among the votaries ".[8] This alone can explain why a *pumś-chalī* or harlot has been associated with Ēka-Vrātya in the well-known Vrātya hymn of the Atharva-Veda. Further, if this Vrātya cult was thus associated with some pre-historic form of Śiva depicted with *ūrdhva-mēḍhra,* it stands to reason why phallic stones, smaller and larger, should have been found in the Indus Valley, some representing naturalistic *liṅgas,* because the *liṅga,* as a matter of fact is the *ūrdhva-mēḍhra.*

Though Śiva with *ūrdhva-liṅga* is not, as a rule, found in Ancient India except in the case of Lakulīśa whether in northern or southern part of the country, the case is entirely different in regard to Eastern India. Here we find almost no exception, says Mr. Amalananda Ghosh rightly, whatever the variety of the image may be : whether it is *Naṭarāja, Kalyāṇasundara, Pārvatī-pariṇaya* or *Ardhanārīśvara,* the *ūrdhva-liṅga* is prominent. But in other parts of India, this libidinous characteristic is rarely met with.[9] This may be due to the fact that in this part of India, the Vāmāchārī cult had always been strong. To cite only two instances, at Pahāṛpur in Bengal one sculpture was excavated representing the offering of *halāhala* or deadly poison to Śiva where the god is depicted standing but with *ūrdhavaliṅga.*[10] Even in an ordinary representation of Umā-Mahēśvara, where things should have been different, the male consort is shown with *ūrdhva-liṅga,* as e.g., in a sculpture found at Chauduar in Orissa.[11] In fact, one of the numerous names of Śiva is *Ūrdhva-liṅga,*[12] and this characteristic of the divinity is preserved almost intact in Behār, Bengal and Orissa, and that too in his various forms, up till the thirteenth century A.D.[13] In South India the Guḍimallam icon is the only instance where the *ūrdhva-mēḍhra* is seen in a form of Śiva other than that of Lakulīśa. It is strange that in South India are to be seen also the horns with which the Mohenjo-daro prototype of Śiva is decorated. " In many religions, especially in those of antiquity, divinities are frequently represented in statue or image or picture wearing the horns of an animal on the head .... ".[14] And although in India the sharp horns of Brahma-

8. Wilson, *Op. cit.,* pp. 257-58.
9. *I.C.,* Vol. II, p. 766.
10. *A.S.I., An. Rep.,* 1926-27, Pl. XXXIII (b).
11. *Memoirs A. S. I.,* No. 44, Pl. VII (2).
12. *Mahābhārata,* XIII, 17, 46.
13. For further instances, see Mr. A. Ghosh, *I.C.,* Vol. II, p. 766, *n.* 3.
14. *Encyclopaedia of Religion and Ethics,* Vol. VI, p. 792.

ṇaspati are referred to in a hymn and also the horns of Agni who is sometimes characterised as a bull,[15] no image of any Indian god was for a long time found wearing a head-dress with a pair of horns. However as early as 1928 in his *Pallava Architecture*, Part II, which forms No. 33 of the *Memoirs* of the Archaeological Survey of India, Mr. A. H. Longhurst writes as follows: "These trident heads were set up in the shrine cells in place of the usual Śiva *liṅgas*. The custom appears to have been peculiar to the Pallavas as such images do not seem to have been discovered elsewhere. They doubtless indicate some special Śaiva cult that flourished during this period ....".[16] It is a pity that Mr. Longhurst, when he wrote this, did not know that a prototype of the historic Śiva was just then discovered at Mohenjo-daro. Otherwise, he would also have concluded that the pair of horns meeting originally in the head-dress of this divinity is found preserved in Śiva even as late as the sixth or seventh century A.D., and in such a remote region as the Chingleput District of the Madras Presidency just as the *ūrdhva-mēḍhra* of the same god is distinctly traceable in his icons of the mediaeval period in East India.

There yet remains the third class of Vrātyas to be noted, namely, the Gara-girs, which means 'the swallowers of poison.' This naturally reminds us of one aspect of Śiva, namely, Nīlakaṇṭha, who became 'blue-throated' because he swallowed the deadly poison called *halāhala*, which was churned out of the ocean. This is doubtless the *Paurāṇik* way of explaining how Śiva became Nīlakaṇṭha. Originally, however, the god must have been credited with swallowing poisons. Even to this day there are some votaries of Śiva, who take delight in showing their indifference to worldly objects, by eating and drinking not only ordure and carrion[17] but also poisonous acids and nails. The Pañchaviṁśa-Brāhmaṇa has therefore aptly described them as eating commoner's food as if it was worthy of being eaten by Brāhmaṇs.

The above three classes of Vrātyas have no doubt been mentioned in the Pañchaviṁśa-Brāhmaṇa. But whether, as a matter of fact, the Gara-girs were in existence in the Saṁhitā period we do not know. There was, however, hardly any difference between the Hīnas and the *Śama-nīchā-meḍhras*. The difference was only in regard to the position of the *mēḍhra*. We may thus take it that

15. *RV.*, I, 140; VIII, 49; X. 155.
16. p. 18, and Pl. XVI.
17. Wilson, *op. cit.*, pp. 233-34.

both these forms of the Vrātya cult were known in the time of the Atharva-Veda. Further, it can scarcely be seriously doubted that the votaries of this cult are the same as the Śiśna-dēvas referred to twice in the Ṛig-Veda. Thus Ṛig-Veda VII. 21. 5 has: *sa śard-had=aryo vishuṇasya jantōr=mā śiśnadevā api gur=ṛitaṁnaḥ*, "let the true god (Indra) subdue the hostile rabble; let not those whose god is phallus approach our sacred ceremony." Again, Ṛig-Veda X. 99. 3 may be thus rendered: "On most auspicious path he goes to battle; he toiled to win heaven's light, full fain to gain it. He seized the hundred-gated castle's treasure by craft, unchecked, and slew those whose god is phallus." If we put the two Ṛiks together, the impression we obtain is that Śiśna-ḍēvas were most probably the Vrātyas who were so well settled in some parts of north-west India that they had castles with a hundred gates. In fact, their settlements have been called Vrāti, as we have noted above. We have also seen that their social structure consisted of the Arhants and the Yaudhas, corresponding to the Aryan divisions: the Brāhmaṇs and the Kshatriyas. It seems that in this case the Vaiśyas were constituted by the people of the province whom they conquered and over whom they ruled. And further as they had a cult and culture of their own, they were a power which the Aryans had to count, though they had a natural abhorrence for the libidinous rites of the Vrātyas. The question that now arises is: were they indigenous to India; if not, from where did they come? The clue to the answer of this question is furnished by the term Māgadha, who, we have seen, is associated with Ēka-Vrātya along with Puṁśchalī. What does Māgadha mean? It has been generally translated by 'a panegyrist, a bard.' Possibly this is the secondary sense of the term. It appears also tempting to connect this Māgadha with Magadha, South Behār, and say that this associate of the god was a native of this country. But South Behār was known as Kīkaṭa in the time of the Ṛig-Veda and Prāchya in the Brāhmaṇa period. Besides, it is doubtful whether any Indian province was known as Magadha in the time of the Atharva-Veda. It is true that Atharva-Veda V. 22. 14 which is intended to be recited for driving away *takman* or fever has: *Gandhāribhyō Mūjavadbhyō=ṅgebhyō Magadhebhyaḥ* | *praish-yan janam=iva śevadhiṁ takmānaṁ paridadmasi*: "To the Gandhāris, the Mūjavants, the Aṅgas, the Magadhas, like one sending a person a treasure, do we commit the fever." But the Paippalāda recension has *Kāśībhyō Mayēbhyaḥ* instead of (A)-*ṅgēbhyō Magadhēbhyaḥ*. It is thus by no means certain that the two contiguous Indian provinces of Aṅga and Magadha were known in the Atharva-Veda period. On the other hand, it is worthy of note the Vishṇu-Purāṇa (II. 4. 69-70) in its description of the people of Śāka-dvīpa says: *Magāś=cha Māgadhāś =ch=aiva Mānasā Mandagās=tathā | Magā Brāhmaṇa-bhūyishṭhā Māgadhāḥ Kshatriyās=tu te*: "The Magas are mostly composed of Brāhmaṇs, the Māgadhas are the Kshatriyas........" The reading *Māgadhāḥ* occurs not only in the Bombay edition of the Purāṇa but also in Wilson's translation of the same. It will thus be seen that the Māgadhas constituted the Kshatriya class in Śākadvīpa. Similarly, the Bhavishya-Purāṇa[18] speaks of the sun worship having come to India from Śākadvīpa and associates Magadha Brāhmaṇas with that worship. It seems that there were Māgadhas staying outside India and in Śākadvīpa. Śākadvīpa has with pretty accuracy been identified with Sogdiana; at any rate, the latter was included in the former.[19] The river Ikshu, which according to the Vishṇu-Purāṇa flowed through Śāka-dvīpa, seems identical with the Oxus which, according to Ptolemy, separated Sogdiana from Baktriana. It appears that Māgadha, who is connected with Ēka-Vrātya, was a priest of the Māgadha tribe emigrated from Śākadvīpa. If this line of reasoning is worthy of any consideration, it seems that the Vrātya cult which afterwards developed into Śivisṁ, originally came to the Indus Valley with the immigration of the Māgadhas from outside India.[20]

To return to our original point, what does the Vrātya hymn of the Atharva-Veda indicate? It indicates the lofty spirituality of the Aryan culture which sublimated the lewd and repulsive features of the Vrātya cult before it was absorbed into Brahmanism and developed into Śivism. This explains why the *puṁśchalī* of the original cult has been described as Śradhā, the Māgadha or priest identified with the Vedic god Mitra, and so forth. Even the *Ūrdhva-mēḍhra* which was phallic in origin was sublimated into Liṅga as a symbol of Śiva and ceased to be naturalistic and repugnant to the fine taste. Well might the French savant, Barth, exclaim: "Of all the representations of the deity which India has imagined, these (*liṅgas*) are perhaps the least offensive to look at. Anyhow, they are the least materialistic...... ".[21]

18. *Brāhma-Parvan*, Chap. 117, v. 55.

19. *J.A.S.B.*, Vol. LXXI, Pt. I, p. 154.

20. This curiously agrees with the fact that the associates of Śiva, the Maruts, have been called Śāka in two Ṛiks (V, 30.10 & VI. 19.4).

21. *Religions of India*, p. 262. Prof. Nilakanta Sastri also has drawn our attention to this (*The Cultural Heritage of India*, Vol. II, p. 23).

The Vrātyas have disappeared as a race doubtless in consequence of the superiority of the Aryan civilisation and of the four Vrātya-stōmas prescribed for converting them to Brāhmanism. In the time of the *Manusaṁhitā* (X. 20-23), they were known simply as *Sāvitrī-paribhrashṭa*, that is, those whose thread ceremony was not performed. As the thread ceremony was celebrated among the three higher castes, naturally there were Vrātya castes not only among the Vaiśyas but also among the Kshatriyas and the Brāhmaṇs, which have been specified in that law book. Thus the term *Vrātya* came to have an entirely different signification. So far as I know, the word *Vrātya* has now survived only in the Marāṭhī tongue in the sense of "naughty, unmanageable, playing pranks."

Let us here pause and reflect for a while upon the results produced by the impact of the Aryan, upon the non-Aryan, cultures in India. We have seen that Ārya was the name of a race and that their faith was the Manu cult. Even about the beginning of the Christian era the ethnic name is clearly traceable in Arianē, one tribe of which is the Arioi after whom doubtless the province must have been so called. Even as late as the tenth century, inscriptions speak of a people called Ārya which was settled somewhere in the Jodhpur State. Such was the might and glory of Aryan culture and civilisation that whichever people came in contact with them either espoused their religion or were at any rate steeped in Aryan culture to such an extent that Vedic Sanskrit became the medium of their thought. Whatever foreign tribes came in touch with the Aryan and did not embrace their rites and faiths were unceremoniously dubbed with the designation of Dāsa or Dasyu, which was originally the name of the Dahaea on the Russian Steppes but was afterwards employed to denote people who practised alien faiths. Even in India when the Aryans obtained a footing and were being settled, they for a time applied the same term, namely, Dāsa or Dasyu, to men of a dusky skin who did not espouse the Brahmanical faith. But before long that term was replaced by another, namely, Śūdra, which also was originally the name of an alien tribe. Śūdra now stood exactly in the same position to Ārya that Dāsa or Dasyu did in the Ṛigvedic period. Aryan culture was spreading apace among the non-Aryan tribes, and the result of it was that Vedic Sanskrit, which was to begin with, the vehicle of expression with them for the purposes of culture, now dominated their vernaculars to such an extent that they were transmuted into what are called Sanskritic languages which are at present spoken over nearly two-thirds of India. Most of the non-Aryan peoples were content with adopting Vedic Sanskrit as their medium of thought, and even imbibing Aryan culture. They were thus Aryanised, though not Brahmanised. Some of them, though they were very few, such as the Asuras, had become full-fledged Aryans and were completely merged into the Aryan population even in the Ṛigvedic period. In the Brāhmaṇa period, however, the Vrātyas who followed an exotic cult were not only Aryanised but also Brahmanised, absorbing themselves and their worship of Śiva into Indo-Aryan population and culture. Later when Śūdra replaced the term Dāsa or Dasyu to denote a non-Brāhmanised people, there were many foreign tribes who were dubbed Śūdra even though they adopted the Aryan culture to a large extent. Such were the Śakas and the Yavanas who were called Śūdra by Patañjali though they could eat food from an Aryan's plate and could even perform sacrifices. It seems that they did not adopt the *Varṇ-āśrama-vyavasthā* and were for that reason relegated to the Śūdra class.

The account hereupto given of the spread of Aryan culture relates to the area occupied by the Aryans in the Ṛigvedic epoch. This area, as we have seen above, comprised not only the north-west part of India but also Afghanistan, Arachosia and eastern part of Iran. But how far east in India did they spread? They had certainly conquered the plains of Sirhind and Ṭhānēsar, as is clear from the frequent mention of the Sarasvatī and Dṛishadvatī. They had advanced as far east as the Ganges and the Jumna, as these rivers also are referred to in the Ṛig-Veda. The Sarayū is also mentioned. But it is doubtful whether it is the Sarayū in Oudh or some river in the west, somewhere in East Afghanistan. Even supposing that the Aryans did advance as far east in India as the modern Sarjū, they seem to have made greater progress towards the south and south-east as is clearly indicated by the mention of the Matsyas and the Chēdis. The former occupied much the same territory as that covered by the modern Alwar, Jaipur and Bharatpur States of Rājputānā, and the latter the modern province of Bundelkhaṇḍ.[22] Though these are the eastern boundaries of Aryandom in the Ṛigvedic period, it must not be supposed that the Aryans had no knowledge at all of the other parts of India. Thus they knew about the wealth and treasures of the sea in the south, and the Kīkaṭas or the people of Magadha

22. *Carmichael Lectures*, 1918, pp. 52-53.

in the east.[23] Aryanisation spread like wild fire in the different parts of India, but Brahmanisation could not make much headway in East India. It was only in the time of the Śatapatha-Brāhmaṇa that the Aryans pushed themselves forward to the east of the Sarasvatī under Māthava, the Videgha, who "carried Agni Vaiśvānara in his mouth," his priest being the Ṛishi Gotama Rāhugaṇa.[24] They went beyond the Sadānīra or the Great Gaṇḍak, and settled down in the country east of it which was called Vidēgha after the clan name of the king. Thus by 900 B. C. Vidēha or North Behār was Brahmanised. But, as I have shown elsewhere, Magadha or South Behār and Puṇḍra and Vaṅga or West and East Bengal were not Brahmanised before the third century A.D.[25] They were certainly not so about 400 B.C. as the Baudhāyana-Dharmasūtra (I. 1. 2. 14) distinctly lays down that "he who has visited the (countries of the)........Puṇḍras........Vaṅgas, Kaliṅgas (or) Pranūnas, shall offer a Punashtōma or Sarvapṛishṭhi"[26] by way of purification. But Magadha, Puṇḍra and Vaṅga were Aryanised much earlier. They were the centres of Buddhism and Jainism. And we know that the founders and teachers of these religions carried on their preachings among the people of these countries by means of a speech—Māgadhī or Prākṛit which was an offshoot of the Vedic Sanskrit. Besides, for some of their doctrines and speculations they were indebted to Brahmanical philosophers also. Why then did Brahmanism take such a long time to spread and dominate this part of the country ? From what quarter could they have encountered opposition to the dissemination of Brahmanism ? Elsewhere[27] I have attempted to give a reply to this question and stated that East India was at this early period dominated by the Prāchyas who had a culture and civilisation of their own which resisted very strongly and for a long time the inroads of Brahmanism. Did they have any socio-religious fabric of their own ? Certainly they have been described as Vṛishalas who were known uptil the time of Manu (X. 43), who speaks of them as follows: *Śanakais=tu kriyā-lōpād=imāḥ kshatriya-jātayaḥ | Vṛishalatvaṁ gatā lōkē brāhmaṇ-ādarśanēna cha* || "But in consequence of swerving from sacred rites and failure to see Brāhmaṇs, these

23. *Vedic Index*, Vol. I, p. 159.

24. *Carmichael Lectures*, 1918, p. 14 & *An. Bhand. Ori. Res. Inst.*, Vol. XII, p. 104.

25. *An. Bhand. Ori. Res. Inst.*, Vol. XII, pp. 110 *ff*.

26. *Ibid.*, p. 109.

27. *Ibid.*, pp. 113 & ff.

Kshatriya tribes have gradually become Vṛishalas." 'These Kshatriya tribes,' of course, include the Pauṇḍrakas. What however we have to understand from this verse is that the Vṛishalas are those who do not observe the Brahmanic ceremonies or do not requisition the services of Brāhmaṇs. In other words, they are a people who are utterly uninfluenced by Brahmanism. In this and the following verse Manu describes the Kshatriya Vṛishalas. That there were Brāhmaṇ Vṛishalas also is clear from what Medhātithi comments on Manu VIII. 16, namely, *tasmāch=chhrāddha-kālē Vṛishalair=na pravēshṭavyaṁ hantavyo vṛishalaś=chaura=ity-ādy=āsu kriyāsu mithyādarśi Brāhmaṇa=eva vṛishala-śabdēna grahītavyaḥ*. From this it is clear that a Brāhmaṇ, if he holds heretical doctrines, may be looked upon as a Vṛishala and should not be invited to a Śrāddha ceremony. This reminds us of the fine of 48 *paṇas* which Kauṭalya (III. 19. 20) says should be imposed upon those who feast Vṛishala recluses such as the Śākyas and the Ājīvakas on the occasion of performing religious rites connected with gods and manes. Vṛishala here cannot mean simply Śūdra, because many of the recruits gained by the Śākya sect at least were Kshatriyas and Brāhmaṇs. It may denote a socio-religious fabric comprising the Brāhmaṇ, Kshatriya, Vaiśya and Śūdra after the pattern of the Aryan community, but above all denotes a man who neither performed Vedic rites nor revered Aryan Brāhmaṇ priests. This may be seen also from Patañjali who contrasts Brāhmaṇs from only Vṛishalas thus: *Brāhmaṇā ime Vṛishalā imē* (Vol. I. 252.17-18), *Brāmaṇasya śuklāḥ (dantāḥ) Vṛishalasya kṛishṇā (dantāḥ)* (1.413.10), *Brāhmaṇasya uchchaiḥ (āsanaṁ) Vṛishalasya nīchair=iti* (I.414.9), and so forth. It is worthy of note that in these and many other instances from the *Mahābhāshya*, Vṛishalas are contradistinguished from the Brāhmaṇs, and not from the Kshatriyas or Vaiśyas. It seems that Brāhmaṇ here denotes, not any Brahmaṇ caste, but, rather the community who observe Vedic ceremonies under the auspices of the Aryan Brāhmaṇ priests, and Vṛishala those who are unbrahmanised and non-Vedic worshippers. In this connection it is worthy of note that in the Pāli Vasalasutta,[28] Buddha has been contemptuously addressed by the Brāhmaṇ Agni-Bhāradvāja as Muṇḍaka, Śramaṇaka and Vṛishalaka. Vṛishala is here the name of the community, Śramaṇa of the religious order contained in it and Muṇḍa probably a section of this order who were shavelings, so that the three epithets could very well be made applicable to Buddha. Nay, even

28. *Sutta-nipāta*, I. 7.

the term Śramaṇa is contrasted with Brāhmaṇ in the Samāhāra-dvaṁdva compound *Brāhmaṇa-śramaṇam* under Pāṇini's Sūtra *Yeshāṁ cha virodhaḥ śāśvatikaḥ* (II.4.9). The Śramaṇas thus were an unbrahmanised non-Vedic sect of recluses. It also appears that the people of East India uptil the third century A.D. had a socio-religious fabric of their own though in some points of culture they were Aryanised. They were generally designated Vṛishala though the term had a contemptuous signification with the followers of Brāhmanism. Their recluse sects were called Śramaṇa and were divided into a number of sections such as the Śākyas, Ājīvakas, Nirgranthas and so forth. They had many features in common. Suffice it to say, Vṛishala was the name of the community to which they belonged. It further deserves to be noticed that in the *Mudrā-Rākshasa* of Viśākhadatta, Kauṭalya addresses Chandragupta Vṛishala, not once, but several times. Vṛishala could not have here been used in a bad sense at all. From a religious point of view, a Vṛishala could not have been held in respect by the followers of Brahmanism, but he suffered no social ignominy on that account at all. It seems that the members of the Maurya dynasty were Vṛishalas in this sense. Thus Chandragupta, the founder, was a Jaina, his grandson Aśoka, a Buddhist; Saṁprati again a Jaina, and Śāliśūka a Buddhist. None of them was a Brahmanist. In fact, if we turn our attention to the history of India prior to the rise of Śuṅga power, what do we find? We find that Brahmanism received no royal patronage at all. The Śuṅgas, we know, were preceded by the Mauryas, the Mauryas by the Nandas, the Nandas by the Nāgas, and so forth. Yet we do not find a single king amongst them who performed any Brahmanical rites and sacrifices which constituted real Brahmanism. Real Brahmanism did not penetrate East India before the rise of the Śuṅgas, but Puṇḍra and Vaṅga, West and East Bengal, was not really brahmanised before the third century A.D. The stubbornest opposition to the spread of Brahmanism in this part of India was offered by the Vṛishalas who had a civilisation of their own, exhibited in the religious domain, principally, by the Śramaṇa sects who had many tenets in common which were unbrahmanical. Time prevents our going deep into the matter. But their common characteristics may be brought to a focus in some such form as follows: belief in *karman* and transmigration and pessimism consisting of bitter complaints about old age, disease and death harassing the beings and the consequent worthlessness and transitoriness of earthly life. The cause of all this suffering is *tṛishṇā*, 'thirst,'—the insatiable desire that drives the beings on to every new *karman* and new rebirths. The remedy is *Ahiṁsā*, 'abstaining from hurting' and *Maitrī*, 'love for all creatures,' leading to the tranquility of the saint and sage, and the consequent emancipation from Saṁsāra, 'the eternal round of rebirths and re-deaths'. All these ideas are never met with in the Veda and scarcely in the Upanishads. In later times they penetrated into the Brāhmaṇ-ridden circles. To take one instance, the *pitāputra-saṁvāda* in the Śānti-parvan (Chap. 175) of the Mahābhārata, comprises a well-drawn contrast of the Āśrama ideal of the Brahmanism advocated by the father with the Renunciation ideal of the Śramanism espoused by the son.[29] The Vṛishala culture has played almost as important a part as the Aryan in the work-a-day Hinduism of to-day.

29. Max Müller's *Hibbert Lectures*, pp. 351 & ff.; J. Muir's *Metrical Translations from Sanskrit Writers*, pp. 28 & ff.

LECTURE V

BRAHMANISATION.

In the course of these Lectures I have more than once remarked that to become a full-fledged Aryan a foreigner had to adopt the *Varṇ-āśrama-dharma.* The Varṇas were by no means crystallised in the early period as they are at present. But to be a member of the Brahmachārī *āśrama* is to be a student of one Veda or another and also of the Vedāṅgas auxiliary to it. Besides, to be a member of the Gṛihastha *āśrama* means to perform the manifold domestic sacraments and also some Śrauta sacrifices occasionally. Thus to fulfill satisfactorily the duties of a Brahmachārī and thereafter of a Gṛihastha meant that you could not do without the help of a Brāhmaṇ teacher and a Brāhmaṇ priest. This is what a Brahmanised Aryan denoted. The Aryan Brāhmaṇs were always anxious to secure converts to their faith. Thus to quote a Ṛik already cited elsewhere, Ṛigveda X. 65. 11 has " those very bounteous (gods), mounting the sun to heaven (*and*) spreading Ārya rites over the earth ". The gods have thus been asked to disseminate *Āryā vratā,* i.e., the Ārya rites, all over the world. That means that the Brāhmaṇs were anxious to spread their cult far and wide and invoked the aid of their gods for the furtherance of that object.

We are so much accustomed to hear about the enterprising and proselytising spirit of the Buddhist and Jaina monks that we are apt to think that Brahmanism had never shown any missionary zeal. Is it a fact, however ? Did not the Brāhmaṇs, or, at any rate, any of the hymn-composing families put forth any missionary effort and help in the dissemination of the Brahmanic culture ? We have to note that the ancient Ṛishis were not mere passive innert thinkers, but were active though not aggressive propagators of their faith. Tradition, narrated in the Mahābhārata and Rāmāyaṇa, says that it was the Brāhmaṇ sage, Agastya, who first crossed the Vindhya range and led the way to the Aryan immigration into the south.[1] When Rāma, after wandering for ten years through the Daṇḍakāraṇya, returned to the hermitage of Sutīkshṇa on the Mandākinī (Gōdāvarī), Agastya was already in the south,

1. Mahābhārata, *Vana-P.*, Chap. 104; Rāmāyaṇa, *Araṇya-K.*, canto XI, vs. 85-86 ; *Carmichael Lectures,* 1918, pp. 17 & *ff.*

staying but a few *yōjanas* from it.[2] This is not all. We find him evermore penetrating farther and farther into the hitherto unknown south and Brahmanising the southerners till he reached the ocean, which he is reported to have drunk.[3] Nay, this is admitted by the Tāmiḷ people themselves. They still point to a mountain in the Tinnevelly District, which is commonly called in English, Agastier, that is, Agasty's hill—"Agastya being supposed to have finally retired thither from the world after civilising the Dravidians."[4] In fact, the Ṛishis were in the habit of moving in large numbers and to long distances, especially, in South India, and making their settlements where they performed sacrifices. This is exactly in keeping with what we gather from the Rāmāyaṇa, as just noticed. To the south of the Vindhya there were many Brāhmaṇ anchorites who lived in that part of South India which was comprised between Mount Chitrakūṭa and the Pampā,[5] tributary of the Tuṅgabhadrā and through which flowed the river Mandākinī (Gōdāvarī), and who performed sacrifices before Rāma penetrated Daṇḍakāraṇya and commenced his career of conquest. There was a non-Aryan tribe called Rakshas or Rākshasa who disturbed the sacrifices and molested the hermits and thus placed themselves in a hostile position to the Brahmanical institutions. On the other hand, under the designation of Vānaras, we have another tribe of the aborigines, who allied themselves to the Brāhmaṇs and embraced their form of religious worship. Even among the Rākshasas we know we had an exception in Vibhīshaṇa, brother of Rāvaṇa, who is said to be *na tu Rākshasa-chēshṭitaḥ*, "not behaving like a Rākshasa."[6] There can be no doubt that by Rakshas and Vānara we have to understand some aboriginal tribes. As regards Rakshas it occurs in the Parśvādi-*gaṇa* of Pāṇini and is mentioned immediately after Parśu and Asura.[7] It thus occupies the third place in the Gaṇa and must therefore be taken as being included in it in the time of Pāṇini himself.[8] Rakshas or Rākshasas were thus known in Pāṇini's time as much as Parśus or Persians and Asuras or Assyrians. As regards the Vānaras, the most celebrated of this tribe were Bālin and his brother Sugrīva who were rulers of

2. Rāmāyaṇa, *Araṇya-K.*, canto XI, vs. 27-8; canto V, v. 36.
3. *Ibid.*, canto XI, vs. 37-42.
4. Caldwell's *Grammar of the Dravidian Languages*, pp. 101 & 119.
5. Rāmāyaṇa, *Araṇya-K.*, canto VI, v. 17.
6. *Ibid.*, canto XVII, v. 22.
7. *Gaṇapāṭha*, No. 193.
8. *Bom. Gazet.*, Vol. I, Pt. II, p. 138, n. 4.

Kishkindhā. And even in later times inscriptions speak of a ruling family round about Dhārwār in the Bombay Presidency who describe themselves not only as 'scions of the Bāli race' and 'lords of Kishkindhā, best of towns' but also 'bearing the device of an ape (*kapi*) on their banner.'[9] This token explains why they were designated Kapis or Vānaras. It may be contended that what the Mahābhārata and Rāmāyaṇa teach us is mere legends. It is, however, a mistake to suppose that legends teach us nothing historical. It may be doubted whether Agastya, as he figures in these legends, is a historical personality. But a man is certainly lacking the historical sense, if he cannot read in these legends, the historical truth that Ṛishis took an important but unobtrusive part in the diffusion of Brahmanic Aryan culture, especially in that part of South India inhabited by the non-Aryan tribes called Rākshasas and Vānaras. The old Ṛishis of India were as enthusiastic and enterprising in this respect as the Buddhist and Jaina missionaries and were often migrating with their host of pupils to distant countries. If any historical instance is needed, it is supplied by the Brāhmaṇ *guru* Bāvarin[10] mentioned in the *Sutta-nipāta*. He was originally a teacher of Pasenadi, ruler of Kōsala, who afterwards left Āryāvarta and was settled near a village on the Gōdāvarī in the Aśmaka country in Dakshiṇāpatha. He is described as proficient in the three Vēdas. He had sixteen disciples—all Brāhmaṇs, and each one of them again with his host of pupils. They all bore matted hair and sacred skins, and are styled Ṛishis. With these pupils of his and their pupils' pupils Bāvarin was settled on the banks of the Gōdāvarī to the south of Paiṭhaṇ in the Aśmaka territory, where he performed a sacrifice in which the villagers participated.

Let us proceed one step further and determine whether the texture of the Brāhmaṇ-dominated Hindu Society was in ancient times elastic, or inflexible as it is to-day. The belief at present is that a Brāhmaṇ, Kshatriya or Vaiśya has been a Brāhmaṇ, Kshatriya or Vaiśya ever since the days of the Ṛig-Veda, maintaining his purity of descent intact. It is also believed that Hinduism is a non-proselytising religion, that a Hindu means an individual born of Hindu parents and not converted to Hinduism, and that consequently Hinduism was always a barrier to foreign races being incorporated into the Hindu

9. *E.I.*, Vol. XV, pp. 107-8. See also my article on *Daṇḍakāraṇya* (in the Jha Commemoration Volume), pp. 56-57.

10. *Carmichael Lectures*, 1918, pp. 4-5, 19 & 22.

community. Let us see how far this popular belief is tenable. Let us in the first place find out whether Sanskrit literature itself contains any statements which run counter to this view.

In the Śānti-Parvan (Chap. 296 vs. 12-18) of the Mahābhārata, Parāśara says: "The status of high-souled persons that have cleaned their soul through austerities, O king, cannot be regarded as affected by their low birth. The sages, O monarch, by begetting children hither and thither, conferred upon them the status of the Ṛishi 'through the power of their own austerities'. My grandfather Vasishṭha, Ṛishyaśringa, Kaśyapa, Vēda, Tāṇḍya, Kṛipa, Kākshīvat, Kamaṭha and others, Yavakrīta, O king, and Drōṇa, that foremost of speakers, and Āyu, Mataṅga, Datta, Drupada and Mātsya,—all these, O Vidēha ruler, obtained their respective positions by resorting to austerities, and became established as the knowers of the Vedas through restraint and austerities. There had sprung only four original *gōtras,* O king, namely, Aṅgiras, Kaśyapa, Vasishṭha and Bhrigu. But other *gōtras* came into existence, O king, in consequence of deeds and austerities, and the good people have adopted these appellations." From this passage it is clear that the people of India knew full well, when the Mahābhārata was being compiled, that there were many Ṛishis of low origin who afterwards became conversant with the Vedas and became the founders of reputable *gōtras.* Nay, there is a verse in the Vanaparvan which says: *jātō Vyāsas=tu Kaivartyāḥ śvapākyās=tu Parāśaraḥ | bahavō=nyē=pi vipratvaṁ prāptā yē pūrvam=advijāḥ* "Vyāsa was born of a fisherwoman and Parāśara of a Chaṇḍāla woman. Many others, who were originally not twice-born, became Brāhmaṇs. To take one instance of a Kshatriya becoming a Brāhmaṇ, we have the well-known verse from the *Anuśāsana-Parvan* (XIII. 4. 48) which may be rendered as follows: "Then Viśvāmitra of great religious austerities attained to the state of a Brāhmaṇ. Although a Kshatriya, he became the founder of a Brāhmaṇ family." Similarly, Vishṇu-Purāṇa (IV. 19. 10) has *Ajamīḍhāt Kaṇvād Mēdhātithir=yataḥ Kāṇvāyanā dvijāḥ*: "From Ajamīḍha Kaṇva there was Mēdhātithi from whom (descended) the Kāṇvāyana Brāhmaṇs". Instances to the contrary are not unknown. Thus Vishṇu-Purāṇa (IV. I. 16) has *Nābhāgō Nēdishṭa-putras=tu Vaiśyatām=agamat;* "Nābhāga, son of (Kshatriya) Nēdishṭa, attained to the state of a Vaiśya". Similarly the same Purāṇa (IV. 1. 14) says: *Pṛishadhras=tu guru-gō-vadhāch=chhūdratvam=agamat*: "Pṛishadhra (son of Manu) attained to the state of Śūdra, through the slaughter of the cows and his preceptor". Instances might be multiplied, but what has been adduced is enough to show that caste was an elastic feature of the ancient Hindu social structure and that a Hindu was raised to a higher or degraded to a lower caste in accordance with his deeds. Let us now see how the Brāhmaṇ-dominated Hindu society treated the foreigners, that is, whether they were converted to Brahmanism or were allowed to remain outside the pale of Hinduism. In Chap. 65 of the Śānti-Parvan there is a most interesting dialogue on this subject between Māndhātā and Indra. Māndhātā enquires: "What duties should be performed by the Yavanas, Kirātas, Gandhāras, Chīnas, Śabaras, Barbaras, Śakas, Tushāras, Kaṅkas, Pahlavas, Andhras, Madrakas, Pauṇḍras, Pulindas, Ramaṭhas and Kambōjas and those born of the Brāhmaṇs and Kshatriyas, and men like Vaiśyas and Śūdras—all those who reside everywhere in the dominions? How should kings like myself settle down all these (tribes) who live like Dasyus?" Indra replies: "All Dasyus should serve their mothers and fathers, their preceptors and seniors, likewise those living in hermitages. All Dasyus should also serve the kings. All religious rites prescribed by the Vedas are laid down as their Dharma. They should perform sacrifices in honour of the Pitṛis (Manes) .... and make reasonable presents unto Brāhmaṇs .... They should make presents to Brāhmaṇs at sacrifices of every kind if they desire prosperity. Such a person shall also perform all kinds of *Pāka-yajña* with costly presents of food and wealth. All these acts which have been laid down for the whole world should be done in this case also, O King!" The passage clearly indicates that the Yavanas, Śakas, Tushāras and other foreigners could be incorporated into the Hindu society, following the rites and ceremonies prescribed by the Vedas. How shocking this is to the orthodox community I need not say. But this is entirely congruous with what Patañjali has told us by implication, namely, that Śakas and Yavanas could perform Brahmanical sacrifices and eat food from the plate of an Aryan householder without defiling it.

It may, however, be asked whether there is any good corroborative evidence in support of this statement of the Śānti-Parvan. For this purpose we have to turn to inscriptions and coins, which, being contemporaneous records, are the most convincing authority on this subject[11]. In the cave inscriptions of Western India, we

11. This subject has been dealt with at length in my *Foreign Elements in the Hindu Population* published in *I.A.*, Vol. XL., pp. 7 & ff., of which the following (pp. 59-65) is a summary brought up-to-date.

find Yavanas frequently mentioned as making gifts to Buddhist monuments. Thus we have two Yavanas from Dhenukākaṭa mentioned in the Kārlī Caves,[12] one called Siṁhadhaya (Siṁhadhairya) and the other Dhaṁma (=Dharma). The Junnar Caves[13] speak of three Yavanas, one called simply Chaṁda or Chandra and the other two from the Garta country called Chiṭa (=Chitra) and Irila. There is only one Yavana inscription in the Nāsik Caves,[14] namely, that of the religious-souled (*dharmātmā*) Indrāgnidatta, son of Dharmadēva, who is described as a northerner and a resident of Dattāmitra, a town in Sauvīra according to the Mahābhāshya[15] and founded apparently by the Greek prince Demetrius. All these Yavana names are Indian except perhaps Irila. As these Yavanas or Greeks made gifts to the Buddhist *chaityas* and monasteries, they are presumably Buddhists excepting Indrāgnidatta whose name is typically Brahmanical. But it is well-known that Buddhism left the domestic ceremonies of their followers to be performed according to the Vedic ritual. This is one of the arguments, says R. G. Bhandarkar[16], brought against Buddhism by Udayanāchārya. "There does not exist" says Udayanāchārya; "a religious system the followers of which do not perform the Vedic rites beginning with Garbhādhāna and ending with funeral even though they regard them as *sāṁvṛita*, i.e., as having but a relative or tentative truth." R. G. Bhandarkar correctly points out that *Sāṁvṛita*, i.e., relating to *Saṁvṛiti*, is a Buddhist technical term. Further, it is in the last Lecture that we have pointed that though Brahmanism was slow to penetrate the Prāchya country, that is, Eastern India, it had permeated South India before the beginning of the Christian era. This is clear from the fact that, in the celebrated Nānāghāṭ Cave Inscription, Sātakarṇi, king of Mahārāshṭra, is represented as having performed not only the Aśvamēdha and Vājapēya but also a number of other Vedic sacrifices[17]. Hence Yavanas or Greeks, even though they made benefactions to Buddhist monuments and were presumably Buddhists, were doubtless followers of Brahmanism. If any doubt still remains on this point, it is dispelled by

12. *E.I.*, Vol. VII, pp. 53 & 55.
13. *Arch. Surv. West. Ind.*, Vol. IV, pp. 92 & ff., Nos. 5, 8, 16.
14. *E.I.*, Vol. VIII, p. 90.
15. *Trans. Inter. Cong. Or.*, for 1874, p. 345.
16. *J.B.B.R.A.S.*, Vol. XX, p. 363, n. 9.
17. *Arch. Surv. West. Ind.*, Vol. V, pp. 86 & ff.

a pillar inscription of about the second century B.C. found at Besnagar in the Gwalior territory in Malwā.[18] It records the erection of a *Garuḍa-dhvaja* in honour of Vāsudēva, god of gods, by Hēliōdōra, son of Diya, who had come from king Antalikita (Antalkidas) to the court of king Bhāgabhadra. Hēliōdōra, called Yavana-dūta, 'a Greek ambassador', and his and his father's name, namely, Hēliōdōra and Diya doubtless correspond to the Greek 'Heliodoros' and 'Dion'. He was thus a Greek by extraction. Nevertheless, the fact that he erected a Garuḍa column in honour of Vāsudēva shows that though a Greek, he had become a Hindu and a Vaishṇava. If any doubt is still entertained, it is completely set at rest by the fact that he is actually styled Bhāgavata in the inscription.

If the cultured and civilised Greeks could not but succumb to one Indian faith or another, it is a matter of no wonder at all that the semi-barbarian hordes that later poured into India yielded to the charm of Indian culture and religion. Such were the Śakas, Ābhīras, Kushāṇas and so forth. The Śakas were represented by two Kshatrapa families in the north and two in the south. While the former two had espoused Buddhism, the latter two were followers of the Brahmanic religion. One of the southern families was ruling over the Dekkan, the most prominent member of which was Nahapāna. Inscriptions of his son-in-law Ushavadāta (=Ṛishabhadatta) are found in the Buddhist caves at Nāsik and Kārlī.[19] His wife's name, we find, was Saṁghamitrā. Both Ṛishabhadatta and Saṁghamitrā are indisputably Hindu names. But in one Nāsik Inscription we are distinctly told that he was a Śaka.[20] His foreign origin is also indicated by the names of his father and father-in-law, namely, Dīnīka and Nahapāna, neither of which is an Indian or Hindu name.[21] Nahapāna, again, has been styled a Kshatrapa and is said to belong to the Kshaharāta family. Kshaharāta is a non-Hindu name. Kshatrapa also is not a Sanskrit word, but is an abbreviation of the old Persian title Kshathra-pāvan, which has been anglicised into Satrap.[22] All these things unmistakably point to the alien origin of Ṛishabhadatta, and, in particular, to his having been a Śaka, though his and his

18. *A.S.I., An. Rep.*, 1908, p. 128 & *ff*; *Modern Review*, 1930 (Jan.). p. 18.

19. *E.I.*, Vol. VIII, pp. 78-88; Vol. VII, pp. 57-62.

20. *Ibid.*, Vol. VIII, p. 85.

21. *I.A.*, Vol. XLVIII, pp. 78 & ff.

22. E. J. Rapson, *Cat. Ind. Coins, Andhras, Kshatrapas, &c.*; Intro. p. c.

wife's name are distinctly Hindu. Now, in one inscription[23] Ṛishabhadatta is also called *tri-gō-śatasahasrada,* 'the giver of three hundred thousand kine'. He is further spoken of as having granted sixteen villages to the gods and Brāhmaṇs. He is also stated to have provided eight Brāhmaṇs with the means of marriage at the holy place of Prabhāsa, that is, Sōmnāth Paṭṭan in Kāṭhiāwār; in other words, he incurred the merit of accomplishing eight Brāhmaṇ marriages. And to crown the whole, he is said to have been *anuvarshaṁ Brāhmaṇa-śatasāhasrī-bhōjāpayitā,* that is, to have annually fed one hundred Brāhmaṇs. This reminds us, as R. G. Bhandarkar has aptly remarked,[24] of the grand feast given by Maharaja Scindia in Poona nearly seventy-five years ago. These charities undoubtedly stamp Ṛishabhadatta as a very staunch adherent of the Brahmanical religion. Yet in origin he was a Śaka, and, therefore, a foreigner!

Almost synchronous with the Śakas were the Ābhīras, another foreign horde, which made incursions into India both south and east, and gave their name to the provinces where they were settled. We have already seen that Patañjali speaks not only about *Śaka-Yavanam* but also *Śūdr-Ābhīram.* They certainly ruled over the Dekkan in the third century A.D. as is clear from a Nāsik Cave Inscription[25] which refers itself to the reign of the Ābhīra Īśvarasēna, son of Śivadatta Ābhīra. That the Ābhīras were originally foreigners is clear from the fact that both in the Vishṇu-Purāṇa[26] and the Musalaparvan[27] of the Mahābhārata they are branded as Dasyus and Mlēchchhas in the story which says that Arjuna, after he had cremated the dead bodies of Krishṇa and Balarāma in Dwārkā, was proceeding with the Yādava widowed females to Mathurā through the Panjab when he was waylaid by these Ābhīras and deprived of his treasures and beauties. Even as late as the ninth century A.D. they were notorious for their predatory habits as is evident from a Ghaṭiyālā inscription in the Jōdhpur State[28]. The Ābhīras are, no doubt, the same as the Ahirs of the present day, who are spread as far east as Bengal and as far south as the Dekkan. Most of them are cowherds, but some

23. *E.I.*, Vol. VIII, p. 78, No. 10.
24. *Bomb. Gazet.*, Vol. I, Pt. II, p. 173.
25. *E.I.*, Vol. VIII, p. 88.
26. *Aṁśa* v. *adhyāya* 38.
27. *Adhyāya*, 7, v. 45 & ff.
28. *E.I.*, Vol. IX, p. 280.

have pursued other callings also, and are distinguished in some places from other persons of these callings by the distinctive appellation of Ahir. Thus we have simple Sonārs or goldsmiths and Ahir Sonārs, simple Sutārs or carpenters and Ahir Sutārs, and so forth, existing side by side in Khāndesh, Bombay Presidency[29]. Ābhīra Brāhmaṇs are also reported to be existing in Khāndesh, Gujarāt and Rājputānā.[30] The Ahirs came into India in such large numbers that they gave rise to a separate dialect also.

So long as India, at any rate, North India, was subject to an imperial dynasty, the north-west frontier of the country was well cared for and effectively guarded against foreign incursions. Such was the case when the Mauryas wielded imperial sway over the whole of Northern India including the north-west frontier provinces. But when, after Śāliśūka *alias* Subhagasēna, the Maurya power declined, we find many foreign hordes pouring into India, such as the Bactrian Yavanas, Śakas, Palhavas, Ābhīras, Kushāṇas and so forth. The next imperial dynasty that exercised supremacy over the whole of North India was that of the Guptas during whose tenure of rule India enjoyed respite for about two centuries. But soon after Budhagupta Gupta imperialism began to totter, and it was an easy matter for the restless Hūṇas to penetrate India. When once this commotion was caused, many other foreign tribes immigrated into India along with them, such as the Gurjaras, Chāhmānas, Maitrakas and so forth. It is not the object of this Lecture to go deep and into every detail of this matter. The names of the first two Hūṇa sovereigns have been clearly preserved in inscriptions. But both are non-Hindu names. The first is Toramāṇa, and the second Mihirakula. We do not know whether Toramāṇa had become a Hindu, but Mihirakula was certainly so. On some of his coins[31] we have, on the reverse, a bull—the emblem of Śiva, with the legend *jayatu vṛishaḥ*, "Victorious be the Bull!" A Mandasōr inscription, again, says that he bent his neck to none but Śiva[32]. This shows that he was a Hindu and a worshipper of Śiva. The Hūṇas are, of course, the Huns or White Ephthalites, and consequently foreigners. But by the eleventh century

29. Enthoven's *Tribes and Castes of Bombay*, Vol. I, p. 24; *Bomb. Gazet.*, Vol. XII, p. 39 & n. 10.

30. Wilson's *Indian Caste*, Vol. II, pp. 26, 120 & 177.

31. V. A. Smith's *Catalogue of the Coins in the Indian Museum, Calcutta*, p. 236; E. J. Rapson's *Indian Coins*: Key to Plate IV., No. 21.

32. Fleet's *Gupta Inscrs.*, p. 146, and correction by Kielhorn in *I.A.*, Vol. XVIII, p. 219.

A.D. they came to be regarded as Kshatriyas. Thus an inscription informs us that a Kalachuri king Yasaḥkarṇa married a Hūṇa princess of the name of Āvalladēvī.[33] They are now one of thirty-six standard Rajpūt families.

Another foreign horde, that came into India with the Hūṇa, was the Gujar, sanskritised into Gurjara or Gūrjara. One clan of this race was Pratihāra or Gurjara-Pratihāra. And the imperial family of this clan was the Pratihāra dynasty of Mahōdaya or Kanauj. They have been called Juzr kings by Arab travellers and writers, such as Abu Zaid, Al Masudi and others, and are spoken of as constantly fighting with the Rāṣhṭrakūṭas in the south.[34] 'Juzr' is an Arabic mode of writing the name 'Gujar'. And there can be no doubt that these Arabic writers have thereby referred to the Imperial Pratihāras of Kanauj who, as epigraphy informs us, were constantly fighting with the Imperial Rāshṭrakūṭas of Mālkheḍ. Nevertheless, two of these Pratihāra kings, Mahēndrapāla and Mahīpāla were patrons of the poet Rājaśēkhara, who has in his plays styled them *Raghu-kula-tilaka*, 'Ornament of the race of Raghu', *Raghu-grāmaṇī*, 'the leader of the Raghus', and so forth.[35] It will thus be seen that by the time of Rājaśēkhara, they had not only adopted Hindu names and the Brahmanic mode of worship, but also traced their descent from an epic hero. Now, the late Sir James Campbell has identified Gujars with the Khazars who occupied a very prominent position on the borderland of Europe and Asia especially in the sixth century A.D. Khazar again is called Gazar, Ghyssr and Ghusar which are all different forms of Gujar.[36] Reminiscences of their immigration into India are preserved in the names of the various provinces called after them. Thus we have a tract of land called Gurjistan in the neighbourhood of the White Hūṇa capital, Badeghiz. A modern trace seems to remain in Ujaristan, with the initial G dropped, which is situated beyond Arghandab west of Hazarā. A third Gujaristan is near Ghazni. There are other provinces named after them, which are too numerous to mention. But the three instances we have here

33. D. R. Bhandarkar's *List of Inscriptions of Northern India*, Nos. 1227-28.

34. *J.B.B.R.A.S.*, Vol. XXI, p. 423.

35. *I.A.*, Vol. XL., p. 23 & n.80.

36. *Bomb. Gazet.*, Vol. IX, Pt. I, pp. 471 & ff. How the mind of some Indian scholars is obsessed, over such questions, either with rank orthodoxy or a false sense of patriotism, may be seen from what has been discussed in *I.A.*, Vol. LX, pp. 239 & *ff.* and *An. Bhand. Ori. Res. Inst.*, Vol. XII, pp. 117 & *ff.*

given are sufficient to show that the Gujars came originally from outside India giving names to the provinces which they occupied on their way to this country. Gujars are still found in numbers in the Panjāb, United Provinces, Rājputānā and Central India, but mostly as cultivators or cowherds. The districts of Gujarāt and Gujarāṇwālā in the Punjab are doubtless called after the Gujars who came and settled there. There is also Gujarāt in the Bombay Presidency which must have been named after Gujars. But in this Gujarāt the Gujars have no longer any separate existence as a clan or people. Here there are indications of this tribe having been merged into the Hindu population like the Ābhīras in Khāndesh. We have thus Gujar and simple Vāṇiās or traders, Gujar and simple Sutārs or carpenters, Gujar and simple Sonārs or goldsmiths, Gujar and simple Kumārs or potters, and Gujar and simple Salāṭs or masons.[37] Like the Ābhīras, however, they do not seem to have exerted any cultural influence. We know that the Ahirs profoundly influenced the Marāṭhī of the Khāndesh district of Mahārāshṭra which is known as Ahirāṇi.[38] They have similarly created a Gujarātī dialect of their own in Gujarāt and Cutch.[39] The dialect of the Ābhīras has been referred to even in Viśvanātha's *Sāhitya-darpaṇa*.[40]

By the beginning of the ninth century things were quieting down in North India which was now held by the Imperial Pratihāra dynasty of Kanauj wielding sway as far north-west as Afghānistān. The only difference between the Gupta and the Pratihāra period was that the Arabs had by now obtained a footing in Sind. The Pratihāras, however, had taken every care to prevent foreign aggression whether from Sind and Multān or from Afghānistān. The Pratihāra power very much weakened after the death of Mahēndrapāla II, that is, about the commencement of the eleventh century, with the result that Maḥmūd of Ghazna began his inroads and was followed by other foreign hordes who by this time had become Muslim by faith. Shortly before the foreign invasions began from the 11th century onwards, the Hindu body politique was fast losing the two invaluable qualities of colonisation and proselytisation so indispensable for the self-preservation and continuance of

37. *Bomb. Gazet.*, Vol. I, Pt. I, p. 4.
38. *Ibid.*, Vol. XII, pp. 42 & ff.
39. *Ibid.*, Vol. V, pp. 78-79.
40. *Parichchhēda*, VI, v. 163.

a race or people and its culture. On the other hand, the new foreign invaders who were of Muslim religion were aggressive proselytisers, with the consequence that instead of Muslims being converted to Hinduism, many Hindus became Muhammadans. Hindu Society was now on its trial. Nevertheless, it wonderfully began to tide over this crisis by reclaiming most of the Hindus that were being converted to Muhammadanism. Śuddhi movement in India began, not recently with the Arya Samajists re-converting the Muhammadan Malkāṇā Rajpūts, but in the tenth century with the compilation of the Dēvala-*smṛiti*, Atri-*saṁhitā* and other kindred compositions in support of this re-conversion activity.[41] The most important of these is the Dēvala-*smṛiti*. The sage Dēvala, we are told, was staying on the banks of the Sindhu, when the ascetics and saints approached him and questioned him on the subject of *śuddhi* which is a word used in the Smṛiti itself. "How, O! blessed one", they asked, "may the Brāhmaṇs, Kshatriyas, Vaiśyas and Śūdras, who have been carried away by the Mlēchchhas, attain to purification ?........ Being forcibly made slaves by the Mlēchchhas, Chaṇḍālas and Dasyus they were compelled to commit an impure act, such as (1) the slaughter of the cow and other animals, (2) clearing away or eating the leavings of their food, (3) eating the flesh of the donkey or camel, and (4) intercourse and dining together with their women." Now, who could these Mlēchchhas be ? We have seen that many foreign hordes poured into India, but that they all became Hindus and were absorbed into the Hindu population. The phenomenon of a Hindu becoming a Mlēchchha arose for the first time when the Muhammadans began to invade and penetrate into this country. The phenomenon of a Brāhmaṇ, Kshatriya, Vaiśya or Śūdra being carried away by the Mlēchchhas, being forced to kill a cow, to clear the leavings of their food, and to eat the flesh of a donkey or camel and having intercourse with Mlēchchha women, is possible only in the case of Hindus captured and snatched away by the Muhammadans to their own country. These facts lead to the inference that the Muhammadans had at that time come right down to the frontiers of India or at best conquered and occupied some of the frontier districts, without being able to push their conquests further into the interior. This agrees

41. This subject was first discussed by me in an article entitled "Is Re-conversion to Hinduism permissible ? " and published in *The Calcutta Review*, 1933 October, pp. 33 & ff. The Smṛitis referred to here will be found published in the Volume: *Smṛitināṁ samuchchayaḥ* brought out by the Ānandāśrama Sanskrit Series.

with the fact that the Dēvala-*smṛiti* speaks of Mlēchchha-sabhā in one place and enjoins expiation on Hindus who have touched or remained together for a long time with the Mlēchchhas in such an assembly. We shall not therefore be far from right if we assign the Smṛiti to the 10th century A.D.[42]

The Dēvala-*smṛiti* expressly lays down that everybody, male or female, healthy or diseased, shall perform a purificatory rite, if he or she is from eleven to eighty years old. That this picture of mass *śuddhi* depicted in our Smṛiti is real and not imaginary may be seen from what the Muhammadan historians themselves have written about this matter. The Arabs conquered Sind in 712 A.D. during the Caliphate of Umar II, when many Hindus were converted to Islam. But when Hakim succeeded Tamim as Governor of Sind, says Bilāduri, the Arab chronicler of the early conquests of Islam, " the people of India had returned to idolatry except those of Kassa."[43] But the Hindus of Sind were not content with this. After the recall of Mohammad bin Kasim, the Muslims retained some foothold on the west banks of the river Indus, but, says Sir Denison Ross, " they were in such small numbers that they were gradually merged into Hindu population. In Mansura (the capital of Sind) they actually adopted Hinduism."[44] Even Al-Bērūni (c. 1024 A.D.), the greatest Arab Sanskritist and historian, remarks : " I have been repeatedly told that when Hindu slaves (in the Muslim countries) escape and return to their country and religion, the Hindus order that they should fast by way of expiation, then they bury them in the dung, stale and milk of cows for a certain number of days, till they get into a state of fermentation. Then they drag them out of the dirt and give them similar dirt to eat, and more of the like."[45]

The Dēvala-*smṛiti* prescribes *śuddhi* for women also. For women also were carried away as slaves, not only in the frontier districts but also in the south of India. Thus in 801 A.H. (=1398-

42. There were two Dēvala-*smṛitis*, one which was known, e.g., to Vijñānēśvara and which comprised all the essential constituents of a Smṛiti, and the other the work which is engaging our attention here and which deals only with one subject, namely, the *śuddhi* of the Hindus that had been defiled through contact with the Mlēchchhas. This latter was composed to meet a special emergency created by the advent of the Muslim power whose ardent proselytising activity began to affect Hindu society seriously.

43. Elliot's *History of India*, Vol. I, p. 126.

44. *Islam*, p. 18.

45. Sachau's *Alberuni's India*, Vol. II, pp. 162-63.

99 A.D.) Dev Rai of Vijayānagar, says the *Tawārikh Firishtāh,*[46] invaded the territory of his Muslim neighbour. He was defeated in the struggle that ensued, and 2,000 Brahman girls were made captives by the army of Firoz Shah Bahmani. This compelled the Rājā to sue for peace as the Brāhmaṇs demanded that their girls be restored to them from their Muslim captors. A treaty was at last signed, and the girls were released. Evidently the Brāhmaṇ girls polluted by the touch of the Muhammadans were taken back into the Hindu fold. Can the Brāhmaṇs of Southern India dream of such a thing now? Nay the Dēvala-*smṛiti* considers also the case of women who have been ravished by the Mlēchchhas and have even conceived. Dēvala adopts a very liberal point of view. But he does not stand alone. Because the same view is expressed even by Vijñānēśvara who expatiates on this subject in the same strain in his gloss on Chap. III, v. 265 of the Yajñavalkya-*smṛitī*. There he quotes verses from many Smṛitis to show that a woman can be taken back into the caste even if she is raped by a Chaṇḍāla, Pukkasa or Mlēchchha. If that had not been the view of Vijñānēśvara, he would mercilessly have demolished it as he does in the case of Suttee.[47] In this case he explains away the Smṛiti texts that condemn Suttee and gives his verdict in favour of the custom. But in the case of the ravishment of women, he is in favour of taking them back into the caste and has therefore cited many Smṛiti texts in support of this view. It is thus clear that up till the beginning of the twelfth century A.D., that is, up till the time when Vijñānēśvara lived and wrote, it was considered to be a correct procedure, both in North and South India, to purify a woman abducted by a Mlēchchha.

To recapitulate what we have discussed above, there was a time when any foreigner could become a Hindu. Whatever foreign tribes entered India, they became hinduised and gradually lost into the Hindu masses. Even the self-complacent Greeks, who were proud of their Hellenism and branded all foreigners as barbarians, were glad to become either Buddhists or Vaishṇavas.

46. This is no doubt what Prof. Sri Ram Sharma says on pp. 8-9 in his *Conversion and Reconversion to Hinduism* (No. 2 of D. A. V. College Historical Series). The same thing is repeated in *Calcutta Review,* February 1934, p. 140. But his reference to *Firishta,* p. 311 in the footnote is wrong and incomplete. This should have been Brigg's *trans.,* Vol. II, pp. 374-75. Here the incident has no doubt been referred to, but Brāhmaṇs, and not Brāhmaṇ girls, are mentioned as having been captured.

47. See his gloss on Yājñavalkya-*smṛiti,* I.86.

The state of things continued till the seventh century A.D. when the tide of Islamic invasion broke upon India, and the Hindus themselves were being converted to the Muslim faith. Even when this cataclysm threatened Hindu society, Hinduism began and continued to tide over it for centuries by reclaiming the Hindus that were converted to Muhammadanism. But soon disintegration set in and Hinduism ceased to be virile. The proselytising activity of Hinduism, which was once noted for its overwhelming force and extended sweep, began gradually to ebb and contract till it is now completely extinct, and the belief has grown up that a Hindu to be a Hindu must be born a Hindu and that if he performed any socially heinous act, even unconsciously or through compulsion, he lost his caste for ever and could never become a Hindu.

LECTURE VI

INDIANISATION

In this Lecture we shall set ourselves to the task of illustrating a different phase of Indian civilisation. I have remarked more than once that when two civilisations impinge upon each other, one adopts and imbibes many features of the other according to the degree of its pre-eminence. And it is always interesting to note what features are so absorbed and by what process. Sometimes, however, some of these features are superimposed upon the old civilisation, and it looks as if they too are being absorbed by it. But somehow they are found unassimilable and gradually thrown out till the corresponding features of the old civilisation assert themselves in their pristine form and virulence. Both these elements are traceable in the Indianisation of foreign cultures. In fact, we have already pointed out what constituents of Aryan culture were selected and imbibed by Indian civilisation. We shall now single out one of the Aryan customs and practices which was discarded by Hinduism although it was being foisted upon it for a long time. Perhaps "Position of Woman in Ancient India" would have been a better subject for this purpose from all points of view, because that would have shown what constituents of non-Indian foreign cultures, Aryan and non-Aryan, were adopted and what others thrown out by Ancient India. But this would require at least four Lectures for its proper elucidation and treatment. We have therefore to be content with "the Cow in Ancient India," and here we shall describe that peculiar phase of Indiansation which shows what pabulum of foreign culture Ancient India had tried to gulp but ejected because it was found unassimilable.

We shall turn first to the Vedas, and above all to Ṛig-Veda to determine whether or not the cow was immolated and also to ascertain what position this animal held in the estimation of the people. Ṛig-Veda, X, 91, 14 gives us an insight into the kinds of animals that were slaughtered on the occasion of sacrifices, and may be translated as follows:

"He, in whom horses, bulls, oxen, and barren cows (*vaśā*) and rams, when duly set apart, are offered up,—

To Agni, Soma-sprinkled, drinker of sweet juice, Disposer, with my heart I bring a fair hymn forth."

It will be seen from this Ṛik that bulls and barren cows were sacrificed along with horses and rams; and many such hymns from the Vēdas can similarly be quoted. Nay, of the animals of sacrifice, bulls and barren cows appear to be favourites of Agni, the god of fire. In Ṛig-Veda, VIII, 43, 11, e.g. Agni is called *ukshānna* and *vaśānna*, i.e. 'eater of bulls and of barren cows.' The bulls, again, were killed not only for the purpose of sacrifices but also for food; and there seem to have been regular slaughter-houses kept. This is evident from Ṛig-Veda, X, 89, 14:

"Where was the vengeful dart when thou, O Indra, cleavest the demon ever bent on an outrage?

When fiends lay there upon the ground extended like cattle (*gāvaḥ*) in the shambles?"

Further, it is worthy of note that the ox-hide was in the time of the Ṛig-Veda turned to many uses, and served as the material of various objects, such as a bowstring, a sling, reins, the lash of a whip, or thongs to fasten part of the chariot. In fact, the ox-hide was so commonly used that the word *gō* is often employed synonymously with *charman*.[1]

In the hymns that have been quoted above, the Sanskrit word used for 'cow' is *vaśā*, which, truly speaking, signifies 'a sterile cow.' It, therefore, seems to have been the general practice to sacrifice a cow that was barren. What is to be borne in mind here is the fact that a milch-cow was seldom, if ever, sacrificed, and consequently the sacrificial cow was the sterile cow during the Vedic times, there being apparently no restriction in regard to the slaughter of bulls. In the Atharva-Veda we have a hymn (XII. 4) which insists upon the gift of a barren cow being made over to a Brāhmaṇ as soon as she is discovered to be so: "The sterile cow in her very birth is born for the gods and Brāhmaṇs. Hence to the Brāhmaṇs she is to be given: that, they say, guarantees the security of one's own property."

Next, the slaying of a cow formed a most essential feature of the funeral ceremonies also. Thus Ṛig-Veda, X, 16, 7, has: "(O corpse) put on the armour, which comes from the parts of the cow, (which will protect thee) against Agni; envelop thyself with (her) thick fat." The meaning of this will be clear from *Āśvalāyana-Gṛihyasūtra*, IV, 3, which gives detailed directions as to

1. Macdonell and Keith's *Vedic Index*, Vol. I, p. 234.

what parts of the cow are to be used and how. Thus we have: "Taking out the omentum of the cow called *anustaraṇī* he should cover therewith the head and the mouth (of the dead person), with the verse *Agnēr=varma*" (*R.V.*, X. 16.7), and so forth and so on. In fact, all the various parts of a cow slain were used to cover the corresponding parts of a corpse, with the object of ensuring the unimpeded march of the dead person in the next world. It thus clearly indicates that in the time of the Ṛig-Veda the cow was considered by some to be of great sacramental efficacy. This peculiar combination of the sense of utility with the sacramental efficacy of the cow did not spring up in the minds of the Aryans after they penetrated and were settled in India as the effect of their new environments, but was a feeling which they shared with their Iranian brothers and which they really brought into India. This is seen from the position which she occupies in the Old Avestic literature and even in the mind of the modern Parsi. In the 9th chapter of the Vendidad of the Avesta, the purificatory power of the cow's urine is dilated upon. It is declared to be a panacea for all bodily and moral evils. It is drunk as well as applied externally, as is done by the Hindus also. Urine of the bull or cow, called *nirang*, is brought to orthodox Parsi houses every morning, and a small quantity of it is applied to the face, hands and feet. The milk of it is applied to the face, hands and feet. The milk of the cow was a favourite and universal article of food. And " flesh seems also to have been dressed for eating. Bows were strung with the sinews of the ox."[2] It is thus quite reasonable to hold that the reverence for the cow, as shown in the Vedic hymns cited above, was not something which was new and unknown before and which generated itself in the mind of the Vedic Aryan in his new surroundings but was a feeling which his forefathers harboured and nurtured and which was consequently hereditary.

Although the barren cow was sacrificed and killed even for the sake of ordinary food and the cow-hide was used for various purposes, sacramental and secular, the animal did command an exceedingly high degree of sanctity with some people in those days of yore. Thus in Ṛig-Veda, VIII, 90, we have two verses in praise of the cow. The first of these is as follows:—

Mātā Rudrāṇāṁ duhitā Vasūnāṁ svas=Ādityānām=amṛitasya nābhiḥ |

2. Wilhelm Geiger's *Civilization of the Eastern Iranians* (Trans.), Vol. I, p. 168.

pra nu vochaṁ chikitushe janāya mā gām=anāgam=Aditiṁ vadhishṭha || 15

Translation

" The Rudras' Mother, Daughter of the Vasus, centre of nectar, the Ādityas' Sister—

To folk who understand will I proclaim it—kill not the cow, Aditi, the sinless."

Here the cow is said to be related to the various divinities and has been asked not to be slain at all. Here the word used is, not *vaśā*, 'a barren cow', but *gau* which denotes the cow in general. In this connection it is worthy of note that another word for 'cow' which occurs in the Ṛig-Veda is *aghnyā,* which means 'not fit to be killed, inviolable.' Sometimes this word is used by itself, sometimes as an epithet of the cow. Sixteen times has this word been traced in the Ṛig-Veda, and its masculine form *aghnya* has also been employed thrice with reference to the bull.[3] It seems that even in the Ṛigvedic period the whole of the bovine species was considered inviolable by some composers of the hymns. Who these were it is difficult to say. They must be some pre-Aryan Indians who became Aryanised like the Asuras and the Vrātyas and contributed to the scriptural hymnology of India, for outside India the worship of the cow as a divinity and the inviolability of her person are utterly unknown.

During the period when the Brāhmaṇas were composed, the slaughter of cows seems to have increased. Among the *kāmyēshṭis* set forth in the Taittirīya-Brāhmaṇa, not only the sacrifices of oxen and cows are laid down, but we are even told what kind and description of this animal are to be offered to what deities. Thus we have to sacrifice a dwarf ox to Vishṇu ; a drooping-horned bull with a blaze on the forehead to Indra as the destroyer of Vṛitra ; a black cow to Pūshan ; a red cow to Rudra ; and so on.[4] This Brāhmaṇa notes another sacrifice called *Pañchaśaradīya-sava,* the most important element of which was the immolation of seventeen five-year old, humpless, dwarf bulls, and as many dwarf heifers under three years.[5] We refrain from giving more instances, as those just given are sufficient to show beyond all doubt that cows continued to be killed, nay were killed perhaps in larger numbers, during the

3. Macdonell's *Vedic Mythology,* p. 151.
4. *Taittirīya-Brāhmaṇa* (Bibli. Ind. ed.), Vol. III, pp. 658 & ff.
5. *Ibid,* Vol. II, p. 778.

Brāhmaṇa period. We shall, however, here notice one or two protests, that are to be met with in a Brāhmaṇa and which are the only ones that we have been able to trace in the whole of the Brāhmaṇa literature. They are not protests in the strict sense of the word, but rather exhortations against eating beef. It is contained in the Śatapatha-Brāhmaṇa, III.1.2.21, and is as follows:—

"He (the Adhvaryu) then makes him enter the hall. Let him not eat (the flesh) of either the cow or the ox, for the cow and the ox doubtless support everything here on earth. The gods spake, 'Verily, the cow and the ox support everything here: come, let us bestow on the cow and the ox whatever vigour belonged to other species (of animals); and therefore the cow and the ox eat most. Hence, were one to eat (the flesh) of an ox or a cow, there would be, as it were, an eating of everything, or, as it were, a going to the end (or, to destruction)........Let him therefore not eat (the flesh) of the cow and the ox. *Nevertheless Yājñavalkya said 'I, for one, eat it, provided that it is tender'*" (*h=ōvācha Yājñavalkyō=śnāmy=ev=āham=aṁsalaṁ chēd=bhavat=īti.*) In spite of the inordinate fondness displayed by Yājñavalkya for beef, this passage from the Śatapatha-Brāhmaṇa contains an undoubted exhortation against eating bovine flesh, certainly not on religious, but on utilitarian grounds. The other passage also is an exhortation, not a protest, against sacrificing not simply the ox, but all animals,[6] not so much again on utilitarian as on ethical grounds.

We shall now turn to the Sūtra literature, which comprise "manuals of conduct in domestic and social relations." The first of these is called Gṛihya-sūtras. Here we must confine ourselves only to one or two instances. The name of the *Madhuparka* rite is familiar to every Hindu, and is set forth in the Āśvalāyana Gṛihya-sūtra (I. 24). The personages in whose honour its performance was imperative are a Ṛitvig priest, a Vedic student on his return home, a king and so forth. The most important offering was of *Madhuparka,* whose name has been given to the whole ceremony. It consisted of honey and curds. The householder rinsed his mouth twice, and sipped a little water. A cow was thereafter brought forward and offered to the guest. Having mumbled *hatō me pāpmā pāpmā mē hataḥ,* "destroyed be my sin, my sin be destroyed," he ordered the immolation of the cow, with the word *ōṁ kuru* (accomplish, amen!). But if he chose to let her loose, he repeated *Mātā Rudrāṇāṁ duhitā Vasūnām* etc., just the Ṛik, quoted

6. *Śatapatha-Brāhmaṇa,* 1, 2, 3, 6 & ff.

above, which speaks of the cow as a divinity and as an inviolable creature. Anyhow this rite, ordains Āśvalāyana, is not to be concluded without flesh-meat. On this the commentator remarks: "when the cow was sacrificed, her flesh served food; but if she was let off, another kind of flesh-meat was provided." If we carefully reflect upon this passage from the *Gṛihya-sūtra,* we come to the following conclusions: (1) that those who pertained to the Brahmanic faith were expected to eat meat at least during such an important ceremony as the *Madhuparka*; and (2) that some of them considered it to be a sin to eat bovine flesh. Nevertheless, some of them did partake of it, because it was so required by the religious ceremony handed down from time immemorial. In that circumstance they could wash off their sin by the recitation of the *mantra* (*hatō mē pāpmā,* &c.) referred to above; but (3) that if they could not get over the qualms of their conscience, they were quite justified in eschewing beef in favour of any other meat. This clearly shows that the pre-Aryan Indian feeling of reverence for the cow as a divinity was gradually getting the better of the Brahmanic sense of utility of the animals, because though Madhuparka was accepted by the Aryanised Indians, all of them could not bring themselves to have a cow killed in their honour as they considered it to be 'a sin' (*pāpmā*).

The *Madhuparka* ceremony seems to have been very old and popular. In the Śatapatha-Brāhmaṇa III.4.1. an account is given of *Ātithya* or hospitable reception of king Sōma. "He, the purchased Sōma, truly comes as the sacrificer's guest—to him (is offered) that (hospitable reception): even as for king or a Brāhmaṇ one would cook a large ox or a large he-goat—for that is human (fare offered to guest) and the oblation is that of the gods—so he prepares for him that guest-offering" This extract from the Śatapatha-Brāhmaṇa indubitably points to the conclusion that the ceremony of killing an ox in honour of a guest of distinction was prevalent even in the time of the Brāhmaṇas. Nay, there are indications which prove that it was in all likelihood known also in the Ṛig-Veda period. Madhuparka has been prescribed even in such late works as the Manu (III, 119-20) and Yājñavalkya *smṛitis* (I, 109-10). Yājñavalkya distinctly lays down that a big ox (*mahōkshā*) or a big goat (*mahāja*) is to be immolated on such an occasion, but Manu makes no remarks in this respect. There can, however, be no doubt that Manu meant a bull to be killed for the observance of this rite. For in Chapter III. v. 3 he ordains that the student, who, after completing his term, has become a *snātaka,* shall be honoured with a bull (*gavā*), which commentators have rightly taken to mean *gō-sādhana-Madhuparkeṇa,* 'with Madhuparka which the bull is a means of celebrating.' The killing of ox formed such an essential part of the hospitality to be shown to a distinguished guest that a compound word consisting of two words meaning 'a bull' and 'to kill' respectively was coined to denote a guest. The word is no other than *gōghna,* which, according to Pāṇini, III, 4, 73; means *gāṁ hanti tasmai gōghnō=tithiḥ,* in other words, *gōghna* is one for whom one kills a bull, *i.e.,* a guest.[7]

We now turn to the literature on Dharma, the earlier stratum of which has been represented by the Dharma-sūtras. Vasishṭha (XIV.40) distinctly lays down that "among (domestic) animals those having teeth in one jaw only, excepting camels, (may be eaten)". This category obviously includes the bovine animal, as we shall see it in detail when we come to consider the views of Manu. Vasishṭha, however, makes an exception in favour of milch-cows and draught-oxen, dictated no doubt by the economic exigencies of the state. But he allows their slaughter only for religious purposes, because the Vājasanēyaka declares, says he, that the milch-cow and the draught-ox are *mēdhya* or fit for sacrifice. Curiously, Gautama says nothing about animals having teeth in one jaw only, but lays down (XVII. 30) that milch-cows and draught-oxen shall not be killed. This last statement, however, clearly implies that he allowed the flesh of those cows and those bulls which were not milch-cows and draught-oxen. He thus practically agrees with Vasishṭha. The case, however, is different with Āpastamba who in I.5.17.29 lays a general embargo on the eating of the bovine flesh, but is compelled to allow it even in the case of a milch-cow and draught-ox because like Vasishṭha he quotes the Vājasanēyaka which declares bull's flesh as *mēdhya* or fit for sacrifice. Because beef-eating has been summarily prohibited by Āpastamba, we must not suppose that the cow had become a sacred animal and it was therefore considered sacrilegious to kill her. For in another place (I.9.26.1) he ordains that if a milch-cow or draught-ox is slain without a reason, the same penance has to be performed as that for killing a Śūdra. Haradatta, the commentator, says that a reason for hurting a cow is anger or the desire to obtain meat. And when such a reason does not exist, what is the punishment inflicted upon the killer?

7. In later times, however, that part of the Madhuparka ceremony which related to the killing of the cow became a subject of ridicule. Thus the passage in which Vālmīki's preparation for the reception of Vasishṭha is described by Bhavabhūti in the beginning of Act IV of his *Uttara-Rāmacharita* is noteworthy and affords great amusement.

Only such a small penance as that of killing a Śūdra. And when the animal, be it noted, is neither a milch-cow nor a draught-ox, such a cow or such an ox may be killed with impunity. Does this show that the cow was regarded by Āpastamba as a sacred animal as in modern times? Baudhāyana is better and clearer in this respect, because even for the destruction of an ordinary cow he (I. 10. 19. 3-4) imposes the fine laid down for slaying a Śūdra, that is, one bull and ten cows, but for killing a milch-cow or a draught-ox, the performance of the Chāndrāyaṇa (lunar penance) over and above the prescribed fine.

We now come to the later period of the Dharma or Smṛiti literature. Of the Smṛitis, those of Manu and Yājñavalkya are regarded as the oldest and most important. And we had occasion to allude to these Smṛitis, while we were inquiring into the nature of the Madhuparka rite. It will have been noticed that beef frequently formed an essential part of this ceremony. This conclusion is also in agreement with other prescriptions of these legislators whether connected with the subject of food or sin. It deserves to be noticed that in Chap. V. of his Smṛiti which deals with lawful and forbidden food, Manu nowhere prohibits the use of beef as he would most certainly have done if it had been condemned in his time as it is to-day. On the contrary, in verse 18 of this Chapter (*bhakshyān pañcha-nakhēshv=āhuḥ an-ushṭrāṁś=ch=aïkatōdataḥ*), he like Vasishṭha sanctions the consumption of the flesh of all domestic animals that have teeth in one jaw only, excepting camels. Under the category just referred to come not only camels but also cows. But whereas he has placed restrictions on the former, he has said nothing about the latter. Obviously, therefore, Manu allows the consumption of bovine flesh. This is not the conclusion which a heterodox person like myself draws, but is also what has been deduced by orthodox Pandits like Medhātithi and Rāghavānanda, who have commented on this passage from the Manusmṛiti. Thus the first of these says: *ushṭra-varjitā ēkatōdataḥ gō-vy-aja mṛigā bhakshyāḥ*. And the second has: *ēkatodataḥ ēkapaṅkti-danta-yuktān gavādīn*. It is thus clear that both these commentators agree in saying that cow's flesh for food is allowed by Manu. Secondly, students of Smṛiti literature are well aware that both Manu and Yājñavalkya distinguish between two kinds of sins: (1) *mahāpātaka* or mortal sins and (2) *upapātaka* or minor offences, and that while 'killing a Brāhmaṇ', 'drinking spirituous liquors'[8] and so forth are put by them under the first class, 'slaying

8. *Manu*, XI. 55; *Yaj*, III, 227.

kine'[9] is relegated to the second. This also indicates that these Hindu law-givers do not consider *gō-hatyā* as heinous and inexpiable as it is to-day. It may, however, be asked why slaying kine was considered an *upapātaka* at all if beef was allowed. The reply to this question has obviously to be given in the words of the Āpastamba which we have considered above. *Gō-hatyā* is reprehensible only if a cow is killed without any good reason such as uncontrollable anger or desire to eating her flesh. It will be seen from the above discussion that *gō-hatyā* was not universally considered heinous or inexpiable even till the time of the Manu or the Yājña-valkya Smṛiti. When then it may be asked : did this offence come to be placed under the category of *mahāpātaka* as it undoubtedly is at the present day? We have got the incontrovertible evidence of inscriptions to show that early in the 5th century A.D. killing a cow was looked upon as an offence of the deepest turpitude, turpitude as deep as that involved in murdering a Brāhmaṇ. We have thus a copper-plate inscription dated 465 A.D. and referring itself to the reign of Skandagupta of the Imperial Gupta dynasty. It registers a grant and ends with a verse saying: "Whosoever will transgress this grant that has been assigned (shall become as guilty as) the slayer of a cow, the slayer of a spiritual preceptor, (or) the slayer of a Brāhmaṇ.[10] A still earlier record placing *gō-hatyā* on the same footing as *brahma-hatyā* is that of Chandragupta II., grand-father of Skandagupta just mentioned. It bears the Gupta date 93, which is equivalent to 412 A.D. It is engraved on the railing which surrounds the celebrated Buddhist *stūpa* at Sāñchi, in Central India. This also speaks of a benefaction made by an officer of Chandragupta and ends as follows : *tad=ētat-pravṛittaṁ ya uchchhindyāt sa gō-brahma-hatyayā saṁyukto bhavēt pañchabhiś=ch=ānantaryyair=iti,*[11] "Whosoever shall interfere with this arrangement—he shall become invested with (the guilt of) the slaughter of a cow or of a Brāhmaṇ, and with (the guilt of) the five *ānantarya.*" Here the object of this statement is to threaten the resumer of the grant, be he a Brahmanist or a Buddhist, with the sins regarded as mortal by each community. The *ānantaryas* are the five *mahāpātakas* according to Buddhist theology. They are : matricide, parricide, killing an Arhat, shedding the blood of a Buddha, and causing a split among the priesthood. The *mahāpātakas* with which a Brahmanist is here threatened are only two : viz., the kil-

9. *Manu,* XI. 60; *Yāj,* III, 234.
10. *C. I. I.,* Vol. III (1888), p. 71.
11. *Ibid,* p. 32.

ling of a cow and the murdering of a Brāhmaṇ. The latter is obviously a *mahāpātaka* as it is mentioned as such in all the Smṛitis, but the former has been specified only an *upapātaka* by Āpastamba, Manu, Yājñavalkya and so forth. But the very fact that it is here associated with *brahma-hatyā* and both have been put on a par with the *ānantaryas* of the Buddhists shows that in the beginning of the fifth century A.D. it was raised to the category of *mahāpātakas*. Thus *gō-hatyā* must have come to be considered a *mahāpātaka* at least one century earlier, i.e. about the commencement of the fourth century A. D.

What could be the cause of this complete change in the popular mind in regard to the status of the cow ? How could the view about the inviolability of the person of the cow and the bull completely dominate the Vedic Aryan practice of slaughtering the cow not only for sacrifice but also for food ? How could *go-hatyā* come to occupy exactly the same place in the popular estimation as *Brahma-hatyā* ? About the end of Lecture IV attention has been drawn to the prevalence of Vṛishala culture represented in its religious aspect, by the Śramaṇa sects such as Buddhism, Jainism and Ājīvikism. One notable feature of this culture was *Ahiṁsā*, 'abstention from injury to all creatures'. To take one instance, Buddha like other Śramaṇa teachers was strongly opposed to the slaughter of the animals in general and of cows in particular. Thus Saṁyutta-Nikāya (III. 1. 9) informs us that once a great sacrifice was being arranged for Pasenadi, the Kōsala king. Five hundred bulls, five hundred calves and many heifers, goats and rams were led to the pillar to be sacrificed. On coming to know about it, the Buddha burst out saying: "Aśvamēdha, Purushamēdha, Vājapēya and such fussy rites can never bring a rich result, because diverse goats and sheep and kine are slain. To such a rite never repair the noble seers who walk the perfect way." This is a protest against *hiṁsā* in general. But a protest against cow-killing in particular is contained in the *Brāhmaṇa-dhammikasutta* of the Sutta-nipāta. In this Sutta, Buddha contrasts the profound self-abnegation of the Brāhmaṇs long long anterior to his time with the ever-waxing cupidity of the Brāhmaṇs who were his contemporaries or lived shortly before his time. Some of the concluding verses may be translated here :

"23. And they having thus received wealth wished for a store, and the desire of those who had given way to (their) wishes increased still more; they then, in this matter, having composed hymns, went again to Okkāka ....

25. And then the king, the lord of chariots, instructed by the Brāhmaṇs, caused many hundred thousand cows to be slain in offerings.

26. The cows, that are like goats, do not hurt any one with their feet or with either of their horns, they are tender, and yield vessels (of milk),—seizing them by the horns the king caused them to be slain with a weapon.

27. Then the gods, the forefathers, Indra, the Asuras, and the Rakkasas cried out: 'This is injustice,' because of the weapon falling on the cows.

29. This injustice of (using) violence that has come down (to us), was old, innocent (cows) are slain, the sacrificing (priests) have fallen from the Dhaṁma".

Can there be a more forcible protest against cow-slaughter than this one couched in the language of Buddha? I have also pointed out elsewhere that prior to the rise of the Śuṅgas the greater portion of India was held by the Mauryas, the Nandas, the Nāgas and so forth who were adherents of one Śramaṇa sect or another and not one of whom performed Brahmanical rites and sacrifices which constituted the essence of Brahmanism. It is true that, with the advent of the Śuṅgas to power, there was a revival of Brahmanism. But Buddhism and Jainism had already spread over the whole of India with virulence and thoroughness. They could not but have deeply impressed the mentality of the people and changed their outlook on life to a large extent. It is therefore no wonder if by the fourth century A. D. the killing of the cow was considered to be as heinous a sin as the murder of a Brāhmaṇ, even by the followers of Brahmanism, although it had all along allowed the slaughter of the bovine species for the purposes of sacrifice and food. This ascendancy of the Śramaṇa sects made itself felt on Hinduism from the Gupta period onwards in a variety of ways. If we open e.g. Chapter V. of the *Manu-smṛiti* we shall find the first fifty-four verses devoted to the description at length of 'lawful and forbidden food', where minute details have been given in regard to what kind of bird and animal flesh could be eaten. But the twelve verses following it dwell upon the merits of abstaining from eating meat and are evidently later additions. Two of these have the following: (V. 48) "Meat can never be obtained without injury to living creatures; injury to sentient beings is detrimental to heavenly bliss; let him therefore shun meat." (V. 53) "He, who during a hundred years annually offers a horse-sacrifice, and he, who entirely abstains from meat, obtain the same reward for their meritorious (conduct)." These verses clearly show that the *Ahiṁsā dharma* of the Śramaṇa sects was producing an impression on the followers of Brahmanism and their law books. The same is the case with the shaving of widow's head which seems to have been adopted from the nuns of Śramaṇa sects,—either Buddhism or Jainism. The older Smṛitis, including Manu and Yājñavalkya recommend *Brahmacharya* or celibacy only to the widows. The later Smṛitis, such as Vishṇu and Nārada, recommend either *Brahmacharya* or Suttee.[12] Still later Smṛitis recommend Suttee only. But no genuine Smṛiti entertains the idea of shaving her head. This custom appears to have been adopted at a very late period from the nuns of Buddhism or Jainism who relinquished all dress and all ornamentation and put on ochre-coloured clothes after shaving their heads. The influence of these Śramaṇa sects is far deeper than is generally imagined,[13] because even Buddha the founder of Buddhism and Ṛishabhadēva the originator of Jainism are looked upon as incarnations of Vishṇu by Hinduism.[14]

Nay, the very fact that Gautama Buddha and Ṛishabhadēva are regarded as incarnations of Vishṇu raises the presumption that what is now called Vaishnavism was originally influenced by Vṛishala culture if it was not an actual product thereof. Accord-

12. See in this connection Miss Sakuntala Sastri's article on *Suttee* published in *An. Bhand. Ori. Res. Ins.*, Vol. XIV, p. 222 ff.

13. Nay, a derivative of Śramaṇa, namely, *Śrāmaṇika*, was adopted into Brahmanical literature as in *Vaikhānasadharmapraśna* (Triv. Sk. Series No. XXVIII, pp. 7 and 15) for which reference I am indebted to Mr. V. R. Ramachandra Dikshitar. But as is clear from this work, the Vanasthas or Vānaprasthas who kept up *Śrāmaṇaka* (*-agni*) could be either *sa-patnīkāḥ* or *a-patnīkāḥ*, (I. 7, 1.), whereas the Śramaṇas of the Buddhist, Jaina and Ājīvika sects could not possibly be thought of as *sapatnīkāḥ*.

14. Buddha is mentioned as an incarnation of Vishṇu in the Varāha, the Bhāgavata, and the Agni Purāṇa. But we are not sure of the time when these Purāṇas were compiled. On the other hand, the well-known Bengali poet-saint, Jayadēva, who flourished in the court of the Sēna prince, Lakshmaṇasēna, speaks of Buddha as an incarnation of Vishṇu and admits that he was instrumental in stopping animal sacrifice and spreading the doctrine of *kāruṇya* or compassion broadcast. As regards Ṛishabha he is mentioned as the son of Nābhi and Mēru-dēvī in the Bhāgavata-Purāṇa (V. 3 & 4). This leaves no doubt as to his being the first Tīrthaṁkara of the Jainas. And Verse 20 of Skandha V. and Adhyāya 3 tells us that Bhagavān, to do good to Nābhi, incarnated himself in the womb of Mēru-dēvī.

ing to the Jaina accounts Kṛishṇa was a cousin and pupil of the twenty-second Tīrthaṁkara Nēminātha who pertained to the Harivaṁśa. The teaching of the Tīrthaṁkaras was summed up in abstention from four things: (1) *hiṁsā*, 'injury to creatures', (2) *asatya* 'lying', (3) *stēya*, 'thieving' and (4) *parigraha* 'possession'. And the Chhāndōgya-Upanishad (III. 17. 6) informs us that Kṛishṇa Dēvakīputra was a disciple of Ghōra Āṅgirasa who communicated a new mode of *Yajña* or sacrifice, according to which the *Dakshiṇās* or gifts bestowed upon priests were *tapō dānam=ārjavam-ahiṁsā satya-vachanaṁ* (III. 17. 4). This marvellously agrees with *tapa ārjavam* || *ahiṁsā satyam=akrōdhas= tyāgaḥ* of the Bhagavadgītā (XVI. 1, 2), expounded by Kṛishṇa. It is scarcely reasonable to identify Ghōra Āṅgirasa with Nēminātha. But it is not unreasonable to hold that Kṛishṇa was a pupil of both. Anyway, his teacher Ghōra Āṅgirasa seems to have belonged more to the Śramaṇa than to the Brāhmaṇ school of learning, as he was opposed to the performance of Vedic sacrifices. That Kṛishṇa was a follower of non-Vedic culture is corroborated by evidence of another type. Thus Harivaṁśa tells us that when the Sarad-*ṛitu* or autumnal season was approaching, and the cowherds, in accordance with the prevalent practice of the country, were intent upon celebrating Śakra-*maha*, or 'Festival of Indra', Kṛishṇa vetoed their proposal in the strongest possible language. "Brāhmaṇs perform" says Kṛishṇa "*Yajñas* of hymns. Peasants perform Yajñas of the ploughshare. We are for the *Yajña* of the mountain. Let the forest mountain be worshipped by us. Let the cows be adored by us. Let the gods worship Indra, but let us worship the mountain. I will surely cause the worship of the cows to be celebrated through force (if need be)," and so forth and so on. This made Indra angry, who caused a heavy downpour of rain. Kṛishṇa however saved the cows and cowherds by lifting up Mount Gōvardhana and sheltering them. It may be contended here that this fight between Indra and Kṛishṇa is after all a Paurāṇik myth. Nevertheless, attention may in this connection be drawn to Ṛig-Veda, VIII, 85. 13-15, where we are informed that with ten thousand soldiers Kṛishṇa came to the Aṁśumatī or Jumna and encamped himself there. Thereupon Indra addressed himself to the Maruts: "I have seen Kṛishṇa swiftly moving on the uneven bank of the Aṁśumatī, like a cloud touching the water. Heroes, I send ye forth. Go, fight in battle." So saying Indra overpowered the *adēvī viśah* 'the godless legion', with Bṛihaspati to help him. That may be one version of the result of the battle. But this much is clear that Kṛishṇa was some ruler who fought against Indra, that is, of course the followers of Indra. But what is meant by saying that his forces were *adēvī viśaḥ* ? Sāyaṇa renders it by *adyōtamānāh..........kṛishṇa-rūpā,* of dusky form." The phrase *adēvī viśah,* however reminds us of *adevā Asurāḥ* and *avratā Dasyavaḥ.* It clearly indicates that Kṛishṇa and his tribe did not follow the Vedic mode of worship. It further seems that the hymn quoted above was composed about the end of the Saṁhitā epoch which may have well-nigh coincided with the early part of the Upanishadic period when Kṛishṇa Devakīputra is referred to as a pupil of Ghōra Āṅgirasa. Nay, the name Āṅgirasa itself stamps Kṛishṇa's culture as of an alien character. The oldest name of the Atharva-Veda, we have seen is Atharvāṅgirasaḥ, that is, the Atharvans and the Aṅgirases." And as the late Prof. Winternitz[15] has pointed out, the Atharvans and the Aṅgirases are two classes of prehistoric fire-priests, the first connected with 'holy magic' and dealing with formulæ for the healing of diseases, and the second, that is, the Aṅgirases, with 'black magic' and with curses against enemies, rivals, evil magicians and such like. The lore possessed and handled by these wizard-priests can scarcely be designated Aryan. The culture associated with Kṛishṇa had thus better be described as Vṛishalic than Vedic. Well might Śaṅkarāchārya run down the Bhāgavata system connected with Vāsudēva, on the ground that it was opposed to the Vedas. "Revilement of the Vedas" says he "is noticeable in it, for instance in the passage: 'Śāṇḍilya studied this *Śāstra,* not finding supreme bliss in the four Vedas'" (*Chaturshu Vēdēshu paraṁ śrēyo=s labdhvā Śāṇḍilya idaṁ śāstram=adhigatavān=ityādi-Vēda-nindā-darśanāt*).[16]

Thus comes to a close this series of Lectures connected with some Aspects of Ancient Indian Culture. I do not know whether they are characterised by any originality at all. But I am afraid that in the outspoken utterance of my own views, I may have wounded the susceptibilities of some of my orthodox friends. My object, however, in taking up this course of Lectures was to try and provoke some thought in the sphere of Ancient India. As I have remarked elsewhere, history of Indian, as of any, culture, is a continuous flow like that of the Ganges. We know that this holy river issues from an ice cave in the Himālayas, called Gaṅgōtrī, 13,800 feet above the sea level and falls into the sea after

15. *A History of Sanskrit Literature* (trans. by Cal. Univ.), Vol. I, p. 120.
16. *Śāṅkara-bhāshya* on *Vēdānta-sūtra,* II, 2, 45.

it has had a course of 1,557 miles from its source. It has numerous tributaries and affluents. Nevertheless, the Ganges maintains its identity. Such is the case with the history of Indian culture, which has received many a contribution and affluence at many periods. This culture has no doubt assimilated whatever foreign elements were assimilable, but has preserved its Indian character. No systematic attempt however has been made to study it and disseminate a knowledge of it through the proper channels. This is possible only if the study of Indian culture is made compulsory by all Indian Universities and at almost all examinations with properly graduated courses. Let us see which University takes the lead in this matter of national importance. At any rate, we in the north expect this University to do something in the matter of composing and publishing a history of South India describing the Dravidian culture and civilisation. The University of Madras is the parent of all the Universities of this Presidency and can alone set itself to this colossal task; and it is difficult to find a fitter person than the Professor of Indian History and Archaeology to undertake and execute this stupendous task with the help of his colleagues. May Padmanābha and Tyāgarāja become One in showering their choicest blessings and inspiring this University to transcend in glory the Śaṅgam activity of the Age of Śeṅguṭṭavan Sera!

INDEX